Praise for *Make a Real Living as a Freelance Writer*:

"Make a Real Living as a Freelance Writer *covers everything novice and experienced writers need to know to succeed at freelancing. Jenna's conversational and comprehensive book gives the inside scoop on how to build a SOLID career that pays off emotionally and financially.*"

　　—*Sheri' McConnell, Founder & President, National Association of Women Writers*

"*Jenna Glatzer, the great guru of all things freelancing, leaves no stone unturned when it comes to writing, marketing and selling. If you're freelancing or considering jumping into the freelancing marketplace, she should be your go-to-gal—before you send out your first query!*"

　　—*Julia Rosien, Senior Editor,* ePregnancy *magazine*

"*If you want to crack top markets and put an end to the stream of rejection letters that flows through your mailbox, read Glatzer's book today. Even if you're already cashing lots of checks from publishers, you can forget all those other writing books on your shelves: Glatzer's fresh, timely advice will launch your career to a new level of success.*"

　　—*Diana Burrell, Co-author,* The Renegade Writer: A Totally Unconventional Guide to Freelance Writing Success

Make a
REAL LIVING
as a *Freelance Writer*

How to Win
Top Writing Assignments

Jenna Glatzer

nomad press

Nomad Press
A division of Nomad Communications
10 9 8 7 6 5 4 3 2
Copyright © 2004 Jenna Glatzer

The trademark "Nomad Press" and the Nomad Press logo are trademarks of
Nomad Communications, Inc.
Printed in the United States.

ISBN: 0-9722026-5-x

Questions regarding the ordering of this book should be addressed to
Independent Publishers Group
814 N. Franklin St.
Chicago, IL 60610

Nomad Press, 2456 Christian Street, White River Junction, VT 05001
802-649-1995
www.nomadpress.net

ACKNOWLEDGMENTS

Thank you to everyone at Nomad Press, the best and most personable publishing staff I have ever worked with. Special thanks to my editor, Lauri Berkenkamp, who goes above and beyond her titled role and became my advisor, supporter, and confidante in addition to helping me whip this book into shape; and to Alex Kahan, who kindly welcomed me into the fold, overlooking the fact that I blatantly ignored just about every bit of his submission guidelines.

Thank you to my wonderful staff at AbsoluteWrite.com: Bob Wagner, who screws my head back on straight when it has come unglued; the lovely Laura Wagner, who allows me to pester her husband at all hours; Amy Brozio-Andrews, who is a warm and wonderful human being in addition to being my right-hand woman; and our talented writers, particularly Sable Jak, Mary J. Schirmer, Jennifer Baum, Gaie Sebold, Bill Harper, Chris Joseph, Kimberly Ripley, Angela Booth, Rusty Fischer, Lyne Royce, Blake Snyder, Mridu Khullar, Katy Terrega, RoseEtta Stone, Moira Richards, Wendy Lyons Sunshine, and Betty Winslow. Meryl K. Evans (www.meryl.net), one of my favorite people in the world and a terrific writer, deserves more thanks than I could fit on this page.

The book wouldn't be nearly as helpful without the generous writers and editors who let me interrogate (er, interview) them. You'll find them throughout the book, but I owe particular thanks to Chandra Czape (www.ed2010.com), Kristen Kemp (www.kristenkemp.com), Stephanie Abarbanel, Bob Boze Bell, Todd Raphael, Bobbi Dempsey (www.magazine-writer.com), Patricia Ferguson (www.patriciaferguson.freeservers.com), Jennifer Nelson (www.absoluteclasses.com/Nelson/womenmag.htm), Kelly James-Enger (www.kellyjamesenger.com), Barbara Stahura (www.clariticom.com), Christina L. Hamlett (www.absolutewrite.com/site/christina.htm), Mad Dog (www.maddogproductions.com), and Tina L. Miller (www.tinalmiller.com).

And, to my fellow e-zine and web site editors, who redefine the word "competitors," thank you for inspiring me, supporting me, and all that you do to help writers. Special thanks to Hope Clark (www.fundsforwriters.com), Moira Allen (www.writing-world.com), Christopher Wehner (www.screenwritersutopia.com), Gary McLaren (www.worldwidefreelance.com), Beth Fowler (www.filbertpublishing.com), Victoria Strauss (www.writerbeware.com), Bev Walton-Porter (www.scribequill.com), Apryl Duncan (www.fictionaddiction.net), and Linda Formichelli (www.twowriters.net).

DEDICATION

To my parents, Lori and Mark Glatzer, who always knew I was going to be a writer and never tried to convince me that clown school was far more practical.

And to Jerry and Debbi Warrington, for their beautiful hearts.

TABLE OF CONTENTS

INTRODUCTION

Writing is the hardest way of earning a living, with the possible exception of wrestling alligators.

—Olin Miller

According to a National Writers Union survey in 1995, the median income for freelance writers was only $4,000 a year. Just 16 percent of freelance writers pulled in more than $30,000 a year. Although the study didn't specify, I'm betting that a tiny percentage of those 16 percent earn their livings writing for magazines (the rest are business or technical writers). Daunting, isn't it?

Wait, it gets worse. In 2001, the union conducted a study to find how the market has changed for freelancers over the past four decades. "In real dollars, freelance rates have declined by more than 50 percent since the 1960s," they concluded. "As an example of the generation-long losses, in 1966 *Cosmopolitan* reported offering $0.60 a word, while in 1998 they reported offering $1 a word. In the meantime, the buying power of the dollar fell by a factor of five. So *Cosmopolitan*'s real rates fell by a factor of three. *Good Housekeeping* reported offering $1 a word in 1966 and the same $1 a word in 1998—a full 80 percent decline in real pay."

And yet, I don't believe those studies stopped even one person from entering the freelancing world. After all, for most writers, being a full-time freelancer is a dream come true: writing from the comfort of our own homes, with no boss watching over our shoulders, and actually getting paid for it.

But it's the "getting paid for it" part that makes freelancing such a challenging career. If you plan to make a living as a freelance writer, you have to know more than that 84 percent of writers who aren't earning a living wage. You have to know how to compete with the top 16 percent. To do so, you'll have to learn where to find writing markets and how to study them, write irresistible query letters, make editors fall in love with you, get regular assignments, negotiate, make deadbeats pay up, and more. This book will be your guide.

When I began freelancing, I made many mistakes. I had taken a few writing courses in college, but no one ever taught me how to sell articles and columns. I knew I had the ability to write, but I didn't know where to start.

I went to the library and somehow convinced my librarian to let me borrow most of the writing section. I was very disappointed with what was "out there:" most of the books were outdated, discussing things like how to use correctable tape on a typewriter and using carbon copy paper for invoices.

The few current books didn't offer me much business advice; rather, they were collections of essays about what it's like to be a freelancer, or feel-good fluff pieces.

I wound up learning how to be a successful freelance writer because I was housebound with agoraphobia and didn't have any other way to support myself. Making a living through my words wasn't just a dream for me—it was a necessity. So, in something of a "trial by fire," I dove into my new career head-first. I began by writing for magazines such as *College Bound* and *Video Librarian*, and worked my way up to the likes of *Woman's World*, *Prevention*, *Woman's Own*, *Physical*, *Contemporary Bride*, and *Writer's Digest*. Now that I'm in that top 16 percent, I'm ready to share what I've learned with you so you can get there, too.

By the time you finish this book, you should be ready to compete with established writers. You'll have the insider knowledge you need to figure out what sells to whom, and how to build up and sustain a lucrative career while wearing pajamas. Though the union's study showed that the rates haven't changed much, the magazine world itself has changed quite a bit. You are about to learn how to make a living as a writer in *today's* publishing climate, where the Internet rules and stamps are nearly obsolete, and the kinds of articles that earned front-page headlines last decade wouldn't even get short blurbs today.

I'll tell you what's worked for me, and magazine editors and other freelancers will add in their advice and comments whenever appropriate. Please have a notebook ready—you will need it to complete some of the exercises.

As your tour guide, I now advise you to keep your arms inside the bus and enjoy the ride.

Chapter 1

SETTING THE STAGE

Inside This Chapter

- **Getting started**
- **Setting goals**
- **Treating writing as a business**

It took me fifteen years to discover I had no talent for writing,

but I couldn't give it up because by that time I was too famous.

—Robert Benchley

"I Write, Therefore . . . "

So, what's a "real living" anyway, and can a freelance writer really earn one?

Let's be realistic. I'm not stinking rich, and I know precisely one freelance magazine writer who I would say is rich.

But when I was 24 years old, I bought my first house in New York. On a lake. And I own a truck and a boat, pay for my own gut-wrenchingly expensive health insurance, and manage to have enough left over to start investing in real estate, plan for my retirement, eat sushi, and give my fiancé lavish gifts like vintage saxophones and Guatemalan fishing vacations for every holiday. All of that comes from the money I earn as a freelance writer and editor. If I can do it, you can, too.

Freelance writing is not a get-rich-quick scheme, so you must be prepared to put in the hours and hard work freelancing requires before you can command big paychecks. For most people, it's important to keep some kind of a day job while building a freelancing career.

When I refer to freelance writing throughout this book, I'm talking about writing for magazines, e-zines, and newspapers. It's easier to earn money writing copy for businesses—brochures, sales letters, press releases, and so on—but let's face it, would you rather tell your friends that your byline is in this month's *People* magazine, or that you're responsible for the latest junk mail they just tore up?

I chose the former and have never looked back. When other people have complained about recession and lay-offs, I have felt gleefully immune. When they whine about their nasty bosses and gossiping co-workers, complain about waking up at the crack of dawn in winter to find the car battery needs a jump-start, fret about being cooped up in an office on a beach day, being bored by their work, not getting recognized for their efforts, or hitting the glass ceiling, I furrow my brow and nod sympathetically, but I secretly pat myself on the back for the career choice I made.

I'm writing this book with a few assumptions in mind.

I will assume that you already have an excellent command of language, including grammar. If you do not, run out and get yourself a copy of *The Elements of Style* by William Strunk and E.B. White. Most editors will toss your query if you keep confusing "you're" and "your." Likewise, I presume you know well enough to spell check everything you send out, including "informal" emails. Everything you write contributes to the impression an editor has of you.

I will assume you have the discipline and the desire to motivate yourself to work on your writing as a career, not just as a hobby. Full-time writers do not, as some would have you believe, lie back in our lounge chairs sipping margaritas while waiting for the muse to pay a visit. Like all other workers, we must show up and we must produce, even when we don't "feel inspired."

I will assume that the idea of research doesn't make you twitch. In my experience, more than half of being a successful magazine writer is being an excellent researcher.

I will assume that you have a strong enough ego that you won't fall into a bone-crushing depression every time an editor rejects your work. Like death and taxes, rejections are a certainty of the freelance writer's life. Decide honestly whether or not you can hack it.

And finally, I will assume that you're actually a good writer.

You're wasting editors' time, as well as your own, if you start pitching ideas before you're confident that you can deliver a well-written article.

If you know you're good, you can't fathom not writing, you read magazines voraciously, and have a strong curiosity about the world around you, you might have what it takes to be a freelance writer. But your potential and your classroom studies are not enough, by themselves, to earn you a career.

"Most people won't realize that writing is a craft," said Katherine Anne Porter, an acclaimed journalist and fiction writer whose work was published from 1922 to 1977. "You have to take your apprenticeship in it like anything else." Her words are as relevant today as they were when she spoke them;

Back to School

How do you know if you're a good writer? Take a writing class. Many colleges offer "continuing education" classes that are not as expensive as mainstream classes. If this is impossible, take an online class or workshop. Make sure you take classes that offer feedback. Find the toughest professor and take his or her class. Ask for brutal honesty. Prepare to do battle with every piece of your brain that isn't ready to become a professional writer yet. Read the magazines you want to target, and decide honestly if your work competes with what's being published. If not, and you want more one-on-one help, hire an editor or writing coach with good credentials and references.

Find writing courses at:

➤ *www.absoluteclasses.com*

➤ *www.writersdigest.com/wds*

➤ *www.writing-world.com/classes*

perhaps even more so because of how competitive the field of magazine writing has become.

Believe it or not, editors want to hire you. They do not relish boomeranging your work back to you with a form rejection letter; most editors are searching for reliable and talented freelance writers, and will gladly hand you an assignment if you can prove yourself. But editors complain over and over that writers haven't done their homework before approaching their magazines. Part of that homework is to learn things like proper format and what belongs on a source sheet, but most important is to read and analyze the work of writers who are doing exactly what you want to do; that is, you must study magazines.

Although some writers have ridiculous beginner's luck and land a national glossy magazine assignment on their first shot, that's not necessarily a good thing. Most writers should get wet in the kiddie pool before they try to swim in the ocean. It can be brutal out there, especially if your swimming skills aren't yet honed. You don't want to land a killer assignment and then have to ask yourself, "Uh-oh . . . what do I do now?"

"The truth is that a lot of people are not ready for prime time, although they may think they are," says Stephanie Abarbanel, senior articles editor at *Woman's Day*. "People send me queries for years and they're just not ready, and then one day they send me something that's just great because they've been writing for smaller markets and they've honed their skills."

Editors at major magazines don't have time to hold a beginning writer's hand, and in most cases, it's presumptuous to expect to start at the top. Don't jump in planning to cut the line. Just jump in and plan to advance quickly.

First, go over your reasons for becoming a freelance writer. What are your goals? To help yourself figure that out, ask yourself these questions:

> ➤ What are the reasons I want to become a full-time freelance writer?
> ➤ What are the reasons I haven't done it already?
> ➤ What are the ways I'm going to get rid of those barriers?

Becoming clear about your goals, what's holding you back, and how you plan to overcome your obstacles can speed up your path to success. For many, the "fear factor" is financial insecurity. Kristen Kemp desperately wanted to write full-time, but wasn't ready to let go of the steady paycheck she earned as an associate editor at Cosmopolitan. So her goal was to earn as much money from her writing as she did from her day job; for her to feel comfortable leaving a staff position, she had to earn $30,000 a year as a freelance writer. She accomplished that in 1999 and has been freelancing for top women's and teen magazines ever since.

For some, the major fear is that they won't have enough ideas to sustain them over a long period of time, or that their current clients won't last, or that

---

Stocking Up

Luckily, a freelance writer doesn't have many start-up expenses, but don't try to skimp on the necessary tools. Your freelancing toolbox should contain the following items:

> ➤ *A computer with a word-processing program that includes spell checking (or access to one)*
> ➤ *A good printer that won't streak*
> ➤ *Copies of several magazines that you'd like to approach in the future*
> ➤ *Stamps and envelopes*
> ➤ *A subscription to www.WritersMarket.com or a current copy of the* Writer's Market *book*
> ➤ *An index card file or a computerized manuscript tracking program*
> ➤ *Computer disks or CDs (to back up all your articles and queries)*
> ➤ *A daily planner*
> ➤ *Internet access: If you have Internet access at home, you don't even need to buy a dictionary or thesaurus; you can find them online at www.onelook.com and www.rhymezone.com, respectively*

they'll break under the pressure of constant deadlines, tough rounds of editing, and too-frequent rejections.

Whatever it is that stands in your way, make it your goal to move it out of the way. As Kristen advises, most people shouldn't quit their jobs "cold turkey" and expect to freelance full-time without any experience behind them. Take your time to build up your credits, your confidence, your bank account, and your skills—but keep that ultimate goal in mind: You are working toward supporting yourself through your writing.

Minding Your Business

Writers who think themselves "artists" should probably stick to poetry and diary entries. If you intend to sell what you write, and to make a living from it, you need to convey an image that does *not* jell with the eccentric, tortured, starving artist cliché. You need to become a businessperson.

What does this entail? Well, if you're thinking about cash, then everything associated with your name must be nothing less than 100 percent clean, clear, crisp, and company-minded.

Clean

Your letters should be neatly typed, neatly signed, neatly folded, and neatly sealed into a neat envelope. Double-check to be sure names are spelled properly, spacing has held up in printing, nothing has smudged, and you've signed the letter. Using bright, floral stationery and envelopes with fun seals will make you look like an artist. Using white or cream-colored matching envelopes and stationary with noticeable, frill-free letterhead will make you look like a businessperson. Believe me; when you receive your neat check, you'll be very thankful if you've come across as the latter.

Clear

Your ideas must be expressed in an organized and easily understandable manner. Whenever you send a letter or make a phone call, you should have all potential questions already answered in your mind. Do not propose a dozen half-baked article ideas. Stick to one or two at a time, and do enough research and thinking ahead of time to be able to explain all the basics without stammering.

You never know when an editor is going to call and ask questions before assigning you a piece. Before *Writer's Digest* assigned me an article about book packaging, then-editor Melanie Rigney wanted answers to several questions: Which publishers use book packagers? How long has this practice been going on? What kinds of books are packaged? What kind of experience does a writer need to break in with a book packager? Because I had done some

> ### The Phone Tone
>
> *When speaking to an editor on the phone, always hang up first. You know the feeling when someone is chewing your ear off on the phone and you really need to get back to your life. Don't be one of those callers. Editors are busy people; respect that. Get to your point quickly, say "thank you," and get out of there.*
>
> *Now, this doesn't mean you can't get personal with an editor. In fact, I wholeheartedly advise that you do . . . but gradually. Do not aim to keep the editor on the phone for fifteen minutes before she's even given you an assignment.*

research ahead of time and was clear about my subject matter, I was able to answer all of these questions with ease, and that resulted in a feature assignment.

Crisp

Part of an editor's job is to make sure you tell your stories in as few words as possible. Let this editor see that her job won't be an uphill battle. Be concise in your correspondence. It doesn't help your cause to throw in everything but the kitchen sink in your query, so if you can possibly pitch your article in one page, do so. If you need more space to truly get your point across, that's fine. Just don't try to write the whole darn article in your query letter.

Company-Minded

When the editor calls you, are there kids crying in the background? Do you have an answering machine message featuring your five-year old singing the "Star Spangled Banner?" When the editor offers to fax you a contract, do you ask her to send it through Kinko's? When she asks you to send an email attachment, do you go to the library and send it through your "Yahoo" account?

Stop it.

These are all signs that you're a person, rather than a business. When you call your car mechanic, you expect to hear machines working in the background, and a person answering, "Dave's Auto Repair. Can I help you?" When an editor calls you, she should expect to hear a business environment, too. If you can't afford (or if it doesn't make financial sense now) to have a dedicated business line, at least be sure that when you answer the phone during business hours, you're in a quiet room. Alert your family that when you're on the phone, they are not to pick up, nag you, or turn on loud music. If you have call waiting, be sure that everyone knows that if the line beeps, the call must be answered professionally and turned over to you right away.

Freelancer Jeffrey Zbar says, "I have caller ID, voice mail, a second line for fax. There's no excuse for anything less than professionalism in this line of work. I have no tolerance for home-based workers who tell me, 'I have to go—my husband needs to use the phone.' If you want to get paid as a professional, you have to act like one. It behooves no one if you do this 'little thing on the side.' If you don't take yourself and your work seriously, you're destined to fail."

It's not necessary for you to have a separate fax line, but it is wise for you to have a fax machine that you can turn on when a caller requests it. There are two reasons. First, once an assignment has been made, both you and the editor should want to complete the contract as soon as possible. Why not email? That's the second reason: As of now, the legalities of contracts via email are not clear. Since you can't effectively "sign" anything via email, it's a much better idea to use a fax.

If you decide to freelance full-time, you may wish to incorporate or register your business as an LLC (limited liability company) at some point. This protects your assets by separating your business from your personal properties. If you choose to do this, be aware that it's not always necessary to incorporate in your home state—and it's usually cheaper to incorporate in Nevada or Delaware. You may wish simply to register a business license using an "official sounding" name. For example, I use the name "Absolute Write" for some of my writing work. This serves me a few different ways. First, I establish a corporate identity, which commands more respect and higher pay. When an editor or potential copywriting client receives a proposal from me, it doesn't look like it comes from Suzy Homemaker moonlighting as a freelance writer. It looks like it comes from a company like theirs. Heck, I might even have personal assistants, designers, and secretaries. I don't, mind you, but I might—after all, I do have a company name.

Another benefit of using a company name is that clients can write checks to your business, rather than writing a check to your personal name. It's a simple rule: Businesses prefer dealing with other businesses. It makes psychological sense—if you were buying wedding favors, for example, would you more readily trust that they would be ready on time and in good condition if they came from West Coast Wedding Planners, or from Jane Myers? Which one

---

Free Fax Service

If you have Internet service, you can receive faxes online through a free service called eFax at www.efax.com. It receives faxes for you on your own personal fax number and then sends them to you as email attachments. Very handy! I use mine all the time, which means I don't need a separate fax line.

Sites to See

To find out more about incorporating, visit these web sites:

➤ *www.delawarecorp.com*

➤ *www.delawareintercorp.com*

➤ *www.nvinc.com*

➤ *www.corpamerica.com*

---

invites an image of a professional team of workers with quality control, and which conjures thoughts of a woman sitting in her living room, accidentally spilling juice on a favor, wiping it off and throwing it in your box, letting the dog lick a few, and showing up an hour before your wedding 10 favors short?

To get a business license in most of the United States, all you have to do is visit your county's or state's government offices (call your local town hall if you're unsure), head over to the desk marked "business licenses," and fill out an application. Bring photo ID. They will check to make sure your business name is unique (that no one else in the state has registered it), then your application must be signed in front of a notary public. The whole enchilada cost me about $33 and took about 15 minutes. Then I went to my bank with a copy of the certificate, and opened up a business account.

When choosing a business name, avoid "cute." "When people try too hard to be cute or clever with their names, like 'Writin' Time!' or 'Words R Us,' it sounds unprofessional," says Nomad Press editor Lauri Berkenkamp. Freelancer Mike Sedge, who's published nearly 3,000 articles, uses the business name "Strawberry Media Agency." It's memorable, yet not cloying. Just about any of the words you can think of that relate to writing (scribe, creative, author, writer, words, pen) have been played on to death. You might try a name that has some kind of personal meaning; it might even keep the editor guessing enough to stick in her mind. It could be the name of the street you grew up on, your first word as a child (provided it's something more intriguing than "mama," "dada," or "baba"), your pet's name, or the name of your favorite flower.

The day you decided to be a freelance writer was the day you became a small business owner. Your words are your products, and you're putting a dollar value on your flair for putting these words together. There is no limit to your earnings potential.

Your talent, persistence, reliability, professionalism, work ethic, personality, and research skills will all factor into your income, but a key to financial success is your ability to see yourself as an entrepreneur with valuable products to sell.

Chapter 2
GENERATING IDEAS

Inside This Chapter

- **Generating topic ideas**
- **Refining ideas into article angles**
- **Finding other sources for ideas**

The Big Idea

So, you've studied up on your craft and figured out that you would like to write. Unfortunately, so have about eight gazillion other people on this planet. Therefore, you have to stand out from the crowd. You have to sparkle. How do you do this? Simple. It all starts with "The Big Idea."

The first secret you must learn in this business is that you don't actually have to write the whole article to get a job. In fact, only bright-green novices attempt to write the whole thing before selling it. What you do need, however, is the *idea* for the great story. You will use this great idea to convince editors to pay you to write the whole article via a proposal called a "query letter." (See Chapter 6.)

You can start one of two ways: Either you can come up with an idea first and then find a market to suit it, or you can let your market be your guide and get ideas by studying the magazines you want to write for. For now, let's assume you want to come up with the idea first. In the next chapter, I'll discuss letting the market lead you.

Your Big Idea is all about finding a need and filling it. You don't have to be the world's best writer to make a living selling your words. You need to be resourceful, creative, prolific, and crafty. You must find something worth telling to a mass audience, and convince the "powers that be" that you're the right person to tell it.

So, where will you find this Big Idea? Well, you've heard that adage, "write what you know." That's a wonderful mantra for finding your jumping-off point. You don't need to stick to "what you know" for the specific focus of your story,

> *Source 411*
>
> *There is always a way to track down the subject of an article. Look up the person on www.switchboard.com. Type the person's name (in quotation marks) into a search engine. Call organizations or businesses mentioned in the article. Call the newspaper itself, or email the reporter. If people are not eager to give out the subject's contact information, ask them to pass along your contact information instead.*

but tap into your already huge vat of knowledge to find the story's basis. This is how you will become an expert. Experts are in demand. People with "stories" aren't. What you have to do is sneak your stories into your areas of expertise. For example: Let's say your hobbies and interests include fishing, watching talk shows, and traveling. Good! You are a potential expert in those areas. Jot these things down. Now comes the fun part: brainstorming article ideas based on those topics.

The biggest mistake you can make when pitching your story is to be too general. Never, ever send a letter to the editor suggesting "an article about fishing." Not even "an article about fishing in Florida." This vagueness is not appropriate for short writing. In general, you will be expected to write between 500 and 2,500 words about your topic. You couldn't possibly tell us "all about fishing" in fewer than 2,500 words. What you could do, however, is give us "a comparison of twelve different lures used to catch bass," or "the pros and cons of joining a fishing club," or even "how the moon can tell you if it'll be a good fishing day."

Also, know the difference between a subject and a story. "A subject is, say, pitching a piece on a new art opening," says Scott Freeman, executive editor of *Atlanta Magazine*. "Pitching a story is, say, 'Here's this new art exhibit and wait until you hear the story behind this one particular painting.' A story is something you tell; a subject is something you point out. As a writer, you're expected to know the difference."

Writers sometimes make the mistake of not digging deeply enough into a subject to find its inherent stories. "I'd like to write an article about autism" won't get you anywhere. Once you've determined you want to write about autism, look around and find out what you can tell that hasn't already been reported all over. We know that autism rates are sharply on the rise. How about talking to some experts who can tell us why? How about telling us about the success or failure rate of different early intervention programs? How about some truly innovative treatments that people are trying, or a fundraiser organized by the nine-year-old sister of a boy with autism?

Stealing Ideas From Other Sources

It's perfectly fine to get topic ideas from other magazines, newspapers, television, radio, and so on. The trick is to find stories the editors won't have already seen. Chances are, if you found a story in a national newspaper or on national network news, any editor who can pay you enough to keep food on your table has seen it (or heard about it through scouts), too.

Melissa Walker, who now freelances for magazines like *Glamour* and *New York* magazine, built up her writing clips by hunting down little-known stories. "'Heartwarming Heartland' stories are great for women's magazines, and they're abundant in small newspapers," she says.

"I look on www.newspaperlinks.com for small-town stories and out-of-the-way newspapers. I found one story for *ROSIE* magazine in the Georgetown University paper. It was about a nine-year-old girl who had raised a lot of money for cancer research after her father's death. A new hospital wing was being dedicated in his name because of her efforts—a perfect heartwarming tale. I called the hospital's media relations department to find the family, and they put me in touch with the little girl's mother."

Teen magazines want true stories, too—just ask Susan Schulz, deputy editor of *CosmoGIRL!*. "The as-told-tos, the real girl stories—I can't be finding those," she told freelance writers at an Ed2010 panel (www.ed2010.com). "If you're out there and looking at whatever local newspaper from your hometown, you're going to come across those . . . Find that thing that not a lot of freelancers are pitching."

Don't discount your local television news and radio stations, either. And look for studies published in obscure trade magazines and peer-reviewed journals. Read new (and preferably *not* best-selling) nonfiction books and interesting college textbooks to get ideas.

Freelancer's Bible

Writer's Market is an annual guide published by Writer's Digest Books. It lists guidelines, contact information, and pay rates for more than 2,000 magazines. Pick it up at your bookstore, Amazon.com, or subscribe to their online version at www.writersmarket.com. The online version allows you to search by pay rate: moderate (up to $0.09/word), intermediate ($0.10–0.49/word), advanced ($0.50–0.99/word), and top rates ($1/word and up).

The Hot Topics

Wondering which topics are in highest demand? Here they are:

Animals: Dozens of magazines are devoted to animals (many that didn't make it into *Writer's Market*), but this is a low-paying market, in general—mostly in the $0.10/word range. *Writer's Market* defines that as intermediate rates, which is probably accurate, but sad!

Automotive: The book lists 44 automotive magazines. Of them, eight pay advanced rates and up.

Business and Financial: Of the 43 business and financial magazines they list, 10 pay at least advanced rates.

Child Care and Parenting: Although *Writer's Market* does list many child care and parenting magazines, literally hundreds more (mostly regional) are not listed here. The national ones, such as *Parenting* and *Child*, pay quite well, while the others are better for reprints and syndication.

Entertainment: You might be misled when you see the low pay rates of most entertainment magazines, but don't be fooled: If you can break into a magazine like *TV Guide* or *Premiere*, you can expect about $2 a word.

Health and Fitness: Health and fitness writing is in high demand and pays quite well (many venues in the $1-2/word range). Don't look only at health magazines (like *Health, Shape*, and *Men's Health*), but consider that nearly all consumer magazines will run health-related articles.

Men's: "Laddie magazines," the slang term for men's magazines like *Maxim, FHM*, and *Stuff*, are on the rise and a great market for freelancers—if you can break in!

Women's: Of course, the big women's magazines continue to be the holy grail for many freelancers. Beyond their "how-to" advice on beauty, fashion, health, and relationships, many also carry personal essays, humor, profiles of women (entrepreneurs and volunteers, especially), parenting tips, financial advice, and more.

Home and Gardening: Fifteen of the 72 markets for home and gardening listed in *Writer's Market* pay at least advanced rates.

Travel: Travel writing can also be quite lucrative, and appears on the pages of just about every magazine category: in flight, general interest, parenting, health and fitness, and more.

Children's: It may be fun to write for children's magazines, but most of them don't pay well. Teen magazines, on the other hand, are becoming more high-profile (witness newer magazines like *Teen People* and *CosmoGIRL!*) and pay respectable rates.

Religious: You can find many, many markets for religious articles, but almost none of these markets pays decently. You can also find quite a few markets for confession stories, but again, they are mostly low-paying.

Sex: Writing about sex? You'll have markets galore. Of course there are the sex magazines, but don't forget that both women's and men's magazines, as well as some general interest, psychology, and health magazines, also run articles about sex. The market you choose all depends on the type of story and angle you take, of course.

Sports: And perhaps the biggest section of all in *Writer's Market* is sports, which boasts 25 high-paying markets.

Other Sources for New Ideas

If I had to sit here at my computer and dream up brand-new article ideas out of the sky every day, my brain would have exploded by now. I'm just not that creative. And you don't have to be either.

There are lots of people out there who are dying to give you fresh new article ideas, free. What's the catch? They want to be quoted in your article—and they're not necessarily the kinds of "experts" editors want you to quote.

Press Releases

First, there are the most desperate publicity hounds: the companies who are sending out press releases all over the place. At this very moment, public relations professionals all over the country are doing some of your work for you: They're trying to come up with newsworthy or interesting stories that could land in magazines or newspapers. But, of course, these releases are self-serving. Ms. PR professional would like nothing more than for you to write an entire article about her client.

Most likely, you won't do that. Rather you'll use the idea and possibly interview her client as a source.

Today, I received a press release from a vitamin company about a new Food and Drug Administration proposal to require clearer labels on nutritional supplements. The vitamin company wanted to use this proposal to their advantage: They were going on the record to say that they supported the FDA initiative

Be careful about stretching your base of knowledge too thin. The fact that you played the flute in junior high school doesn't mean you're qualified to write an article about how to play the flute for Musician Today *magazine. What it does mean is that you have an interest and some background information about the topic. It could qualify you to write a profile or an interview of a famous flutist, or to write about the necessity of music programs in public schools.*

and thought the requirements should be even stricter. The company placed a blatant plug in the press release for its own brand of vitamins, of course, and why they're the greatest thing in the history of the galaxy.

As a writer, my job is to be an editor's first gatekeeper. I have to think like an editor for a moment: Would I want to run an article about this company's vitamins? No. They're not paying for advertising space, and there's not much that's interesting about these vitamins in particular. So I'm not going to pitch my editor a replica of that press release, but I could take the idea behind the release and find a way to make it worth space in the magazine.

If the FDA proposal mentioned in the press release passes, that topic might be a great story for *Men's Fitness*. This magazine's audience is very interested in nutritional supplements, and part of the magazine's mission is to educate its readers about what will promote better health.

I used that release as a starting point, then went to the FDA's web site and read its own fact sheets on the topic. Sure enough, there was a story there. A lab discovered that many supplement companies lie about the ingredients in their products, and the FDA found contaminants in many supplements.

Will I end up interviewing anyone from the vitamin company? Maybe. Unlikely, actually, considering that those with commercial biases rarely pass muster as experts. But they'll have my undying appreciation for providing me with a great story idea.

Editors and other freelance writers are inundated with the same press releases that you'll find, so seek a better way to use the same information: Be the first person to pick up on the story and pitch it, look for very old releases (at least a year old) and find out if anything new has happened in the intervening time, or dig deeper than anyone else into the topic—think of a new angle. Most freelancers won't go much further than reading the release, doing a little research, then pitching. You can delve into those dark recesses of your brain to

---

Sites to See

Search around on the Internet for press release sites, and you'll find that many of them will even email you new releases in your categories of interest. Once you've dealt with public relations agencies, they'll also send you their releases personally, especially if you tell them what kinds of topics interest you. Try these:

➤ *www.prnewswire.com*

➤ *www.prweb.com*

➤ *www.ereleases.com*

think of an angle that no one else will have thought to pitch, package it with other material, or find a way to pitch it to a market that most people won't associate with the story right off the bat.

For example, most writers who read a press release about a new study on PMS will think of women's magazines. You, on the other hand, could think of a way to spin this into a story for men: How to better understand your woman when she's gone hormone crazy. Or "Is it PMS, or is Your Lady Just a Mental Case?," an article that would delineate what behaviors can really be attributed to PMS, and which ones can't. It could even be a funny little filler for a pregnancy magazine about why pregnant women should be happy they don't have to deal with PMS.

You can also ask experts for their brief comments about a particular release. If you found a provocative study that says children raised by gay couples have more disciplinary problems than other children, you could send a note to gay activist groups asking for their response to this (mentioning that you're looking for story ideas). Maybe they'll, in turn, point out the reasons the study is bogus, or they'll tell you about other studies showing that children raised by gay couples are smarter, happier, and higher achievers. This is all grist for the mill; instead of just pitching an article based on that study (as many writers will), you can now pitch a completely different article sparked by what you found in response to that study.

Dig. That 84 percent of freelance writers who aren't earning a living wage aren't diggers. Those top 16 percent know how to turn over rocks and dig through dirt to find a story. It's up to you to uncover that great story before anyone else does, and to present it as a well-packaged gem that will make an editor's eyes light up. Take that initiative and contact people—by phone, email, fax; however you can reach them—and ask them for their stories.

Now you need to learn how to connect with the people who will *buy* your article.

ASSIGNMENTS
Getting the Idea Process Started

 Assignment 1

Write down a list of any and all topics that interest you—it's okay to be general. Here are some ideas to get you started.

Think through your whole day. Don't neglect anything. What do you do from the moment you wake up until the moment you fall asleep? You turn off your alarm clock. (An article about alarm clocks disrupting valuable sleep stages! Or waking up to music versus waking up to that annoying beeping sound. Or the optimal number of times to press the "snooze" button.) You brush your teeth. (Article: "What all those touted ingredients—fluoride, peroxide, baking soda—really do for your teeth.") You take a shower. Maybe with your significant other. Lucky you. ("Romantic showers for two.")

Then you go to work. This is the most obvious area of expertise. Let's say you're a secretary. "How voice recognition software can save you from repetitive stress injuries." "How to avoid screaming at your boss when he's a total idiot." "Five couples (or ex-couples) share their wisdom about dating in the office." Think about what cover story would entice you to pay three dollars for a magazine. You don't have to have the information to actually write the article yet. You just have to know you can get this information later.

Next, you come home. What happens? Do you have kids? Great! You'll find a wealth of article ideas. You could write about childcare agencies, potty training, decoding teenage slang, teaching table manners . . . you're getting the idea now, right? Run with it!

There are markets for almost any conceivable topic. Don't limit yourself to the headlines you read in *Vogue* and *Good Housekeeping*. Between newspapers, consumer magazines, trade magazines, e-zines, tabloids, literary journals, and more, you're bound to find an appropriate publication for your Big Idea.

Assignment 2

If you're coming up short, fill in these blanks and find out the many ways you're already an expert.

My age: _____

My hobbies:

_____

Every school I've ever attended:

_____

I've taken lessons in:

_____

I've visited/lived in:

_____

I've worked as a:

_____

My religion/spiritual practices:

_____

My musical/sports interests:

_____

My heritage:

_____

My pets:

_____

I know how to:

_____

My friends are interesting because:

_____

My family is interesting because:

_____

I collect:

_____

I am passionate about:

_____

When friends describe me, they tell people I am:

_____

In my life, I have overcome:

_____

If I could have learned one lesson earlier, it would be:

_____

I spend most of my money on:

_____

Awards and honors I've won:

_____

Look at all the ways you're already an expert! These are all possibilities for articles and essays.

From this list or your own brainstorming, write at least one page of general topics that interest you, then weed out the most interesting ones. Narrow it down to three or four. Then write those three or four topics on top of brand new pages (you can use the worksheet that follows). Now fill up those pages with specific article angles. Just write. Don't edit yourself. Don't judge. Just write whatever pops into your head. If you need motivation, play it like a game of Scattergories. Set a timer for 10 minutes. See how many ideas you can jot down before the timer sounds.

My Topic Worksheet

	Topic One	Topic Two	Topic Three
General Topic	*Cats*		
An angle I could use	*Feline diabetes*		
More specific	*How to know if your cat has it*		
Variations on that angle	*How to treat it, special diets*		
A second angle I could use	*Therapeutic value of cats*		
More specific	*How cats react to human hormone imbalances*		
Variations on that angle	*Do cats relieve stress?, cats used in prisons or mental hospitals*		
An angle that's so ridiculous I can't believe I wrote it	*How witches use cats in wacky rituals*		
A funny angle	*Mating like a tomcat*		

In the Topic One column, over "Cats", the word SAMPLE appears as a watermark.

	Topic One	Topic Two	Topic Three
A serious angle	*How domestic cats evolved from wild cats*		
A men's angle	*What you can learn about your woman from her cat*		
A women's angle	*Celebrities' cats*		
A teen or children's angle	*Evolution of cartoon cats (Heathcliff, Garfield, Bill the Cat, Hello Kitty)*		
An angle I've never seen before	*How children project their fears onto pets*		
An angle I've seen, but can twist	*Cat people versus dog people*		

Once your brain has opened up to this kind of idea generating, you'll be amazed by how much more perceptive you'll become in general. Conversations you overhear will trigger ideas for new articles. An event you witness in a parking lot will trigger another. Moments before drifting off to sleep, you'll think of your most compelling idea ever.

And then you'll have forgotten it in the morning.

Even if . . . no, *especially* if you think there's no way you'll forget this one. The solution? Keep a small notebook and pen next to or under your bed, possibly with a flashlight, for those bedtime flashes of brilliance.

Chapter 3

FINDING MARKETS

Inside This Chapter

- **Print markets vs web markets**
- **Researching market sources**
- **Obtaining guidelines**

What Are the Markets and What Do They Pay?

If you're looking to make a substantial living as an article and/or essay writer, there are three types of markets to concentrate on: consumer magazines, trade magazines, and e-zines. What about newspapers? Keep them on the back burner—the way back burner, except when you're looking to build up your credits in the beginning, or when you're looking to resell something you've already had published. Although newspapers can be as competitive as magazines and the assignments can be just as difficult, their pay rates are abysmal; it's rare to find a newspaper that pays more than $0.10/word, and most community newspapers have to be convinced to pay at all.

Consumer magazines are meant to appeal to mass audiences, and are not targeted to a specific industry or career. They can be general interest (like *Time*), targeted to a wide but particular audience (like *Redbook*), or devoted to special interests (like *Tattoo* magazine). These include the national glossy magazines in grocery store check-out lines, convenience stores, bookstores, and doctors' offices. But there are other, smaller consumer magazines that you'll find in your airplane seat pocket, pet store, the gym, your pharmacy, or even at your favorite casino. This is the area most writers try to break into. Pay varies quite a bit, from nothing at all to $3 a word (and sometimes even more).

Any publication that focuses on a particular occupation or industry is called a trade magazine or journal. There are trade magazines for almost every kind of work, from art dealers to truck drivers. This is where your expertise can shine. In general, your written eloquence is not as important as your research and timely knowledge. These publications are easier to break into than consumer magazines, provided you can prove "expertise" in a particular area. Writers often overlook trade journals, but if you're a good researcher, you can find steady assignments and good pay by tapping into the trades. For example, *Workforce Management*, a magazine for human resources executives, pays up to $1.50 a word and isn't inundated with submissions. *Boardwatch*, a trade magazine for the telecom industry, pays $1 a word.

E-zines are magazines on the Internet. The only major differences between print and online magazine articles are that online articles tend to be shorter and more informal, and include hyperlinks (links to other web sites containing pertinent information). The most popular sites (Slate.com, Discover.com, and Wired.com, for example) pay quite well, and some others might surprise you: Lifetimetv.com pays $1 a word, and TheKnot.com pays $0.75 a word, for instance. Topics stretch as wide as your imagination. This is a nice way to build up your credits, and can also provide you with steady assignments. Whereas most magazines are published monthly, many e-zines are weekly (or even daily), so they need more articles and columnists than their print brethren.

If you're looking to jump-start your career as a fiction writer or poet, your best chance for recognition may come in the form of literary magazines. Often published by colleges and universities, these magazines have a low, and usually regional, circulation. They generally seek scholarly essays, intellectually challenging prose, poetry, and book reviews. These markets don't pay much, if anything. However, what they lack in moolah, they make up in prestige. If you're marketing a novel, book publishers will be impressed if you succeed in

---

The Business Branch

To supplement your magazine-writing income, you may want to venture into writing for businesses, also known as copywriting. This includes advertising copy, speechwriting, press releases, brochures, radio or television copy, slogans, captions, newsletters, memos, reports, media kits, instructions, manuals, and so on. Businesses with an online presence may also use "content providers" (which is just another name for "freelance writers") to write promotional copy, background information, relevant articles, autoresponders, etc. Pay is typically based on hourly or per-project rates, rather than per word, and can be very lucrative. In The Well-Fed Writer, *author Peter Bowerman suggests charging a starting rate of at least $50 an hour.*

placing your work in one of the more prominent journals (*Cimarron Review*, *Ploughshares*, and *Story*, for example), but it won't do much for your nonfiction magazine writing career.

Differences Between Writing for Print and Writing for the Web

Some writers make their entire living by writing for online markets. I used to earn most of my income from e-zines, and now divide my time about evenly between print and online markets. If you're a fan of instant gratification, online writing may be for you, too. While print magazines often have lead times of several months, most web sites will post your work within a few weeks (or even days) of submission.

However, that also means that deadlines are tighter. You'll likely have less time to research and write pieces for the web.

Stylistically, online writing tends to be shorter, snappier, and more irreverent than print counterparts. You must be very concise, since most web surfers click faster than they turn pages—they skim, rather than read. The glare of a computer screen is less friendly to the eyes than the pages of a magazine or book. Your writing must hook them in the first sentence, and if your article drags, your audience will probably stop reading.

Another perk of online writing is the response it generates. According to Steve Outing, columnist for *Editor & Publisher*, "You'll have more interaction with your audience—more email letters; you might participate in online discussion forums after publication, or in live chat sessions with your users. Your users will give you great feedback (more than print readers), and they'll give you lots of tips about what to write about and what they want to know about."

If you're looking for good pay, you should pay attention to corporate web sites (especially if they produce e-newsletters, auto-responders, or news updates) and big e-zines. In general, the more traffic a web site gets, the more you can expect it to pay for writers. Advertisers pay according to traffic, so a site that gets plenty of it should be earning much more than low-traffic sites. Sites sponsored by well-known companies also tend to pay well.

Be aware, though, that some major magazine editors scoff at clips that have been published online. No matter how well you've been paid for it, that article you wrote for SomeBigWebsite.com is probably not going to impress editors at *GQ*. So, online markets can help you build up a readership, learn the editorial process, and make some cash, but they're not the best résumé boosters. They're about on par with small newspapers in many editors' minds. Very few web sites—such as Salon.com, Wired, Slate, and Office.com—are even worth mentioning in your bio. Think of it this way: If the editor is unlikely to have ever heard of the web site you're referencing, she'll assume it's not a decent publication with high editorial standards like hers.

Researching the Markets

There are many ways to find markets that are open to freelancers. Finding places to submit your work is easy if you know where to look.

Of course, your first stop is the *Writer's Market*. The online version at www.writersmarket.com has some extra markets, such as newspapers and greeting card companies, and it's more up-to-date than the print books. When an editor moves, contact information changes, or there's a shift in the editorial needs, online markets guides like this one can make the change immediately, rather than waiting for the next print edition to come out the following year. In addition, you can also use their handy submission tracker, which reminds you what you've submitted where and tells you when it's time to follow up.

Another helpful guide is the *American Directory of Writer's Guidelines*, which prints the guidelines that magazines send to writers verbatim. I wouldn't advise buying this one first; buy *Writer's Market*, and if you have extra cash, buy this one to supplement your efforts. Why? It often doesn't list the important stuff like pay rates, rights, and response time, and half of the guidelines state the

---

Sites to See

Here are a few of the most reliable sources for market information:

➤ *Absolute Markets (www.absolutemarkets.com) puts out a biweekly newsletter that contains U.S.-based and international market guidelines.*

➤ *Writer's Digest (www.writersdigest.com) has a great, searchable database of markets.*

➤ *Writers Crossing (www.writerscrossing.com) provides a free e-book filled with markets when you sign up for their newsletter.*

➤ *Funds For Writers (www.fundsforwriters.com) is a weekly listing of jobs, contests, and grants for writers.*

➤ *Writing-World (www.writing-world.com) offers market guides based on category, plus a free newsletter that includes markets and contests.*

➤ *Worldwide Freelance Writer (www.worldwidefreelance.com) sends out listings of U.S.-based and international markets and sells e-books with links to market guidelines online.*

➤ *Writing For Dollars (www.writingfordollars.com) has a searchable database (not completely current, but useful) and a newsletter.*

➤ *Freelance Success (www.freelancesuccess.com) requires a paid membership, but publishes excellent market guides about high-paying magazines.*

obvious things like "Read the magazine" that you really shouldn't have to read a hundred times over before getting the picture. But each book contains information and markets that the other doesn't have, and by using both, you can get a more complete picture of each magazine or publisher you want to write for.

The next best tools are online, and they are free. The Internet is a fabulous place to find new markets.

Not all sites are equal, though; some market guides online are rarely updated. Whenever possible, look for a date on any guidelines you find online. Newsletters and e-zines that are mailed to your email address tend to be more current than the market lists posted on the web.

You can even run a search for "freelance writers," "writers wanted," or "writer's guidelines" on any major search engine, and you're likely to come up with lots of listings. Try specifying if possible; add words that fit your needs (example: paying markets, romance, teen magazines).

Getting Dirty

There are some magazines' guidelines that you won't find anywhere, so sometimes it's necessary to do some field work and "get dirty" again. If I wanted to write for *Marie Claire*, for example, I won't have any luck tracking down their needs in the *Writer's Market* or online databases.

Some big magazines choose not to be listed in *Writer's Market* or other guides, because they get plenty of submissions already and don't need to encourage more writers. That doesn't mean they aren't open to queries; rather, they know that if they don't let the guides publish a listing about them, then potential writers actually will have to buy the magazine, read the masthead, and, with any luck, read the content. And some of the smaller magazines just aren't on *Writer's Market's* radar.

Keep this in mind: *The Gale Directory of Publications and Broadcast Media* lists more than 27,000 newspapers, magazines, and journals in the United States. Publist (www.publist.com) lists 150,000 magazines, journals, newsletters, and e-zines. *Writer's Market 2004* lists 2,300 of them. That tells you that *Writer's Market* is an excellent starting point, but it shouldn't be your only resource.

There are times when you'll have an idea that's appropriate for a specific magazine that's not listed in market guides. They may not even publish writers' guidelines. This doesn't mean you should give up on them; it just means that you'll have to read the magazine carefully and figure out their guidelines as best you can. See Chapter 4 for a detailed explanation of how to analyze a magazine.

There are other times when you've exhausted your search for a market for a particular query or article in the usual guides and need to find other possible markets for it.

> **Make Money from Markets You've Never Heard of**
>
> *In 2002, I had written a humor essay targeted to brides-to-be. I sent it to all of the decent-paying and appropriate bridal magazines listed in* Writer's Market, *and only two of them responded—both to turn the piece down. But a month or so later, my Air Mail Markets columnist for Absolute Markets (www.absolutemarkets.com) gave guidelines for* Queensland Bride *magazine in Australia. I sent them the essay, and they paid me $300 for it. I forgot about the essay soon after that . . .*
>
> *Until I found allyoucanread.com, that is. You know how many bridal magazines they list? Fifty-seven. Yeah, seriously. Most of them are small, regional magazines, so they don't get listed in the writers' guides. I just sent that humor piece to about 25 of them, more than a year after I thought I had "retired" the piece after only one sale, and quickly made two more sales.*

On www.allyoucanread.com, a terrific web site for magazine and newspaper sources, you can find links to magazines and newspapers organized by location and category.

If you're willing to shell out a few bucks, you may want to buy e-books or subscriptions to sites that cater to your preferred topics. For example, at www.mooseinthebirdbath.com, you can buy an "E-Writing Kit" that contains email addresses for editors at 155 regional parenting publications, and/or 85 niche parenting, regional women's, and niche women's magazines. Be aware that it doesn't contain guidelines or editors' names, but many writers say they've had great luck selling reprints with this guide. At www.sex-writer.com, you'll find more than 100 markets for porn and erotica. And you'll find 500 travel markets at www.travelwriters.com.

Media Bistro (www.mediabistro.com) is an excellent resource to find markets, too. It's free to search their job listings, which include many calls for freelance writers, and some of their articles and news sections are free, too. But the other juicy stuff is part of their paid membership, called the AvantGuild. I recently signed up for an AvantGuild membership and am very pleased that I did. As of this writing, it costs $49 for an annual membership, and you get access to their "How to Pitch" weekly guides, which provide excellent insider information about what editors at high-paying magazines are looking for, along with a range of other features and benefits like chat transcripts from panel discussions, a free web page for your portfolio, and more.

If you're broke, no problem—it'll just require a little more legwork. You might try http://dir.yahoo.com/News_and_Media/Magazines. The obvious first step is to visit the sites, make sure you like the content, and then hunt around for writers' guidelines. They may be in the "Contact Us" or "About Us" sections. But let's say you can't find any guidelines, or even an editor's name. What to do?

Find the best email address you can find. Not the general email box (like info@website.com), if you can avoid it. Not the webmaster, unless that's the only address listed. Instead, look for editor@, or news@, or someone whose name is actually listed. If there's nothing but a general email address listed, use that.

> *Hello,*
> *I have a terrific article idea to pitch for YourMagazine, and I don't know where to send my query letter. Can you tell me who I should contact, or if there are writers' guidelines I can request? I'm an experienced freelance writer and would love the chance to write for YourMagazine. Thanks so much for your time.*
> *Regards,*
> *Jenna Glatzer*

Will the webmaster write back? It's likely. And if he doesn't, you have two options: You can go back to that site and hunt around some more—find another email address, or a mailing address or (last resort) a fax number. If there's a phone number, you can call and make the same kind of statement I made above. Mention you're a writer, and you'd love to send a story pitch, and you'd like to know the appropriate editor's name and where to send it.

Sometimes the writers' guidelines will arrive and mention nothing about payment, or the editor will write back and tell you they don't have formal guidelines, but would be happy to read your query—again, no mention of payment. And since you're a writer who is aiming to make serious money, you can't spend your time researching and working up queries for a market that may be nonpaying or low-paying. Very simply, here's what to write:

> *Thank you for sending the guidelines [or for responding]. I'm eager to send you a pitch. Can you tell me what your average pay rates are?*

ASSIGNMENT
Getting Started

Go back to your trusty notebook and pick out your Big Idea. Pick several markets that seem like they'd best fit your idea. Find as many copies of the magazines as you can: Ask your doctor, dentist, or hairdresser if you can take his or her old magazines. Ask friends if they have already-read magazines you can keep. Swap magazines with other writers. Visit your library and read like crazy. If your library doesn't have the magazines you want, ask if they can do an inter-library loan to get them for you.

Now that you have the magazines, request writers' guidelines, if they are available. Even better—pretend to be a potential advertiser and request a full media kit. This will give you a better idea of the magazine's editorial schedule and plans.

At the very least, visit the magazine's web site. Usually, web sites will have several sample articles and columns online.

Make sure you are researching current issues of the magazine: Don't go through the old boxes stored in your attic to see if you can find a copy of the magazine from six years ago. "Before you get to me you need to do a little homework. People just neglect to do this," says Stephanie Abarbanel, senior articles editor at *Woman's Day*. "*Woman's Day* two years ago is different from *Woman's Day* today. Sit down, go to the library, and look at the last six months of issues. If you send me something that would have been appropriate for the magazine two years ago, I see that you're not paying attention."

Ladies' Home Journal relaunched in March of 2003 with a new editor-in-chief and a whole new editorial focus and tagline: "heart, home and family." Some columns are the same, but there are many new columns too, focusing on true stories and family relationships. Be careful not to pitch an article for a column that's been retired!

Also make sure to send your query to the right editor. "I'm still getting queries for an editor who I replaced seven years ago," Stephanie says. "People are not taking the time to look at the masthead."

Does it matter? You bet it does. You may think, "No big deal, it'll get to the right place," but it's annoying to editors when queries come addressed to their predecessors. Take the time to show the editor respect by making sure you know who's in the driver's seat now. The easiest way to do this, of course, is to look at the masthead of the current issue.

To be even more up-to-date, though, you can visit the following web sites to learn about magazine staff changes:

- ➤ www.mediapost.com (You can also plug the name of the magazine into their "Knowledge Base" and it'll return a list of the people they have tracked from the magazine—including email addresses)
- ➤ www.woodenhorsepub.com
- ➤ www.writersmarket.com (See the "Market Watch" section)
- ➤ www.mediabistro.com/articles/archive.asp?sec=revolvingdoor
- ➤ www.mediamap.com

Gather up all this information in preparation for your big pitch. At the end of this assignment, you should have:

1. At least five potential markets in mind for your big idea.
2. Copies of as many of these magazines as possible.
3. Printed out guidelines from the magazines' web sites, found guidelines in a market guide, or mailed requests for guidelines by email or postal mail.

Got it now? You have your idea, and you've found likely places to submit it? Great! Now it's time to figure out how you're going to convince an editor that your work belongs in her pages.

Big Idea _____

_____

_____

_____

Markets:

1. _____

    ☐ copies of magazine   ☐ writers' guidelines

2. _____

    ☐ copies of magazine   ☐ writers' guidelines

3. _____

    ☐ copies of magazine   ☐ writers' guidelines

4. _____

    ☐ copies of magazine   ☐ writers' guidelines

5. _____

    ☐ copies of magazine   ☐ writers' guidelines

6. _____

    ☐ copies of magazine   ☐ writers' guidelines

7. _____

    ☐ copies of magazine   ☐ writers' guidelines

Chapter 4
STUDY YOUR MARKET

Inside This Chapter

- **Analyzing freelance opportunities**
- **Gaining an edge over competitors**
- **Dicovering clues to what magazines want**
- **Finding sources and ideas for specific departments**

Analyze the Magazine

The most common advice I hear from magazine editors is, "Study our magazine!" But what exactly does that mean?

Studying a magazine is more than just reading the articles. It entails figuring out which sections and departments are open to freelancers, who is the target market, the word count of different types of articles, the magazine's style and tone, and more.

For this exercise, you'll need at least two, but preferably three, recent copies of a magazine. Guidelines are not enough, as you'll soon understand.

I'm going to use *Family Circle* as an example. I've picked up copies of the November 19th and the January 14th issues of the magazine. If I wanted to write for *Family Circle*, I'd know that the first order of business would be to figure out if I had an idea that *Family Circle* might buy. And I'd start with the table of contents.

What do I see? Seven sections: "FC Good Food," "Home and Garden," "Beauty and Fashion," "Health and Fitness," "Family Answer Book," "Good Reads," and "In Every Issue."

My next order of business is to compare the names of the writers with the masthead, so I can figure out which articles were written by freelancers, and which were staff-written. So now I see four entries in the "FC Good Food" section. These are recipes and very short articles and questions and answers about food. The first recipes were written by Donna Meadow. A quick look at the masthead, and I see she's an associate food editor—which means she's on staff, not a freelancer. The other two pages of recipes don't have bylines, which means they're also staff-written. So now I know that I won't pitch *Family Circle* any recipes. That leaves the one page of short articles and Q&As, which is written by Susan McQuillan. She's not listed on the masthead, but she is a nutritionist and registered dietitian, which means she's not a "run-of-the-mill" freelancer. I now compare this to the other issue of *Family Circle*: There are three entries in this section for recipes, and no short articles or Q&As. From this, I now know that I can reasonably forget about landing an assignment in the "FC Good Food" section. No problem; there are plenty of other sections left.

Now I see the "Home and Garden" section. Two articles are listed: one with a byline and one without. The one whose byline is listed is Robin Ruttle, and she's also on the masthead. I look at my other issue and find more of the same, so again, now I know I can cross their "Home and Garden" section off my list.

In "Beauty and Fashion," there's one bylined article and one with no byline. Uh-oh, the bylined article is written by their fashion and beauty director. Forget this section.

In "Health and Fitness," we have three articles, all with bylines. One is written by a doctor who is not on their masthead. The next one's on staff. The last one is a freelancer. Aha! So there is a possibility that I could sell *Family Circle* an article about health or fitness. I compare this to the other issue and find even better news there. Four articles are in the section, and three of them are written by freelancers.

Armed with this information, I now want to take a closer look at the articles written by freelancers.

In the most recent issue, a doctor wrote the article, "Are Health Problems Making You Fat?" and the other freelancer wrote, "Take Inches Off: New 4-Step Workout." What's the common denominator? Both are about weight issues, which is a very hot topic in women's magazines. In the November issue, freelancers wrote, "Stop Smoking Now: A Woman's Guide," "'Crunches Flatten Your Tummy' and Other Fitness Myths," and "Is Your Fridge Making You Fat? 50 Diet Tricks." Are you seeing a trend here? Clearly, *Family Circle* likes ideas about weight loss and looking slimmer.

Now I want to read those articles and check their word counts.

"Are Health Problems Making You Fat?" is a three-page feature article. The article has approximately 2,300 words and two sidebars. Sidebars are the short auxiliary tips, facts, or additional information that's listed in a box or otherwise set apart from the main text of the article. Occasionally staff writers write the sidebars too, but more often, if a freelancer has been hired to write the main article, he or she will also write the sidebar.

The article starts with a Zimmerman lead, meaning that it starts with a story about a person. The person is called only "Janet," and it's a three-paragraph story about how Janet couldn't lose weight, no matter how much she dieted, until she got treated for polycystic ovary syndrome. The rest of the article talks about different health problems that may cause you to gain weight.

"Take Inches Off" is a pictorial exercise guide, listing four steps. It's about 1,500 words. "Stop Smoking Now" is also a three-page feature article with one sidebar. "'Crunches Flatten Your Tummy' & Other Fitness Myths" is a two-page feature with one sidebar. It is a "list article," which means that, like the "Take Inches Off" article, it is written in list format. It lists eight fitness myths and debunks them. This article quotes a few people: a certified personal trainer, a certified exercise specialist, and a research scientist. It also mentions a "recent study" about cortisol levels in athletes who exercise in the morning.

What I have learned through this exercise is if I want to pitch a feature health or fitness article, I know that (a) I have a good chance of landing an assignment about weight loss, (b) I might have success pitching a "list article," (c) articles in this section run about 1500–2500 words, (d) I should have several experts in mind to quote, and (e) I should think of at least one sidebar to pitch with the article.

Is any of this information in *Family Circle's* guidelines? No. That's why studying a magazine is so important.

Now, why would I want to pitch more weight loss articles if they just ran so many articles about weight loss? Because when a magazine has articles about a particular topic again and again, that topic is a tried-and-true success for that magazine.

Sometimes only the lead changes—the headline and the "catch phrase" that sells the article—and the actual content of the article is almost the same as every other article on that topic. For example, a magazine may run an article about "meditation in the workplace," giving its readers tips for ways to meditate while on lunch or bathroom breaks. Three months later, that same magazine might run an article about "making your own guided meditation tapes." Have the principles of meditation changed? No. It's the same basic advice, just presented in a different format and with a different "hook." So take inventory of the most-reported topics, and see if you can come up with a fresh angle and still stay within their framework.

This can work for you and against you. First, it means that there are fewer truly original articles editors will accept, but it also makes it much easier for you to sell rewrites and re-slanted articles. See Chapter 9 for more information about reselling your work.

The real goldmines for freelancers are found in two sections in *Family Circle*: "Family Answer Book" and "Good Reads." Luckily, these are the two longest sections, containing six and seven articles, respectively.

The "Family Answer Book" contains how-to articles and one humor column. What are these articles about? In the January headlines, I find two articles about parenthood, one about psychology, one about spirituality, two about money (making more of it and keeping it safe), and a humor column about how men can use the dishwasher.

The November headlines offer two articles and a humor column about parenthood, one article about psychology ("What Makes Happy People Happy?"), one article about saving money, and one about holiday shopping. So both issues have articles about parenthood, money, and psychology.

Then come the "Good Reads," a mix of human interest stories, personal essays, and tips. The lists in the two issues are almost identical, so here's what I discover:

The **"Women Who Make a Difference"** column profiles volunteers who have had a big impact on their communities. It's about 1,500 words.

"From the Heart" tells a heartwarming, feel-good human interest story, and is about 2,000 words.

"Special Report" is also a human-interest story about people who have overcome great obstacles; in both the November and January issues, these were roundup articles, meaning that they profiled two or more people in one article. About 2,000 words.

"Total Know-How" is two pages of tips aimed to help women with a common problem, like getting organized. In both issues, the articles are arranged as bulleted lists with lots of short tips. 1,500 words plus one sidebar.

"Full Circle" is the last page of the magazine, and it's a personal essay about a topic the readers can relate to, or an opinion piece about a current issue. About 750 words.

These departments are ripe for freelancers. They are tightly focused, so if you take the time to read these pages and get an idea of what sort of articles belong in them, you'll stand a better chance than if you pitch a general feature article.

We can do a similar analysis of *Cosmopolitan*. In their January issue, the top five subjects were fashion and beauty; relationships and sex; celebrities; career; and health and fitness.

On more careful examination, I notice that out of 10 department pieces for "beauty," seven are basically just photo spreads with small blurbs, two are short "how-to" pieces that are staff written, and one is a "Questions and Answers," also staff written. In other words: The fashion and beauty section is not open to freelancers. Forget it. Then I look at the next most-popular section: relationships and sex. Four articles and columns are written by staff members, leaving four articles written by people who aren't on the masthead.

That means there were four opportunities to get your relationships and sex article published in *Cosmo* in January.

Wait. Don't kick yourself for missing this chance. Think about that statistic for a moment. Just generously speculate and say that there are a total of 12 articles by freelancers in this issue. Twelve people got the "nod."

Now think for a moment about how many people sent in queries, made phone calls, and submitted reprints in the course of one month.

Thousands.

Thousands of people were vying for those 12 coveted spots, and the playing field was not even. Big magazines use the same people over and over; writers who they know and trust. Unfair? Maybe not. Think about it this way: Wouldn't you want to do business with someone who's already proven himself? Someone who's already shown he's capable of meeting deadlines, turning in well-written work, documenting sources, and so on?

Be an Overachiever

If you're going to break in at *Cosmo*—or any other major magazine with only a few freelance spots—you're going to have to work harder than their established freelancers. You can't turn in a half-baked pitch, a couple of local clips, and expect an assignment, no matter how great your idea is.

Nicci Micco, nutrition editor at *Self*, told writers at an Ed2010 panel in 2002, "I do have a stable of freelancers that I know are good and I like working with them. So if you pitch me like, 'I want to do the skinny on the strawberry,' I'm going to say, 'Work a little harder! Why should I give that to you when I know that so-and-so is going to turn it in, and we'll change three words and send it to my top editor?'"

Every time an editor selects a new writer, it's a risk. His butt is on the line, because if he hires you and you do a lousy job or miss your deadline, someone

Commercially Viable

Whenever appropriate, mention how your story will appeal to the publication's target audience. It's great to get statistics if you can. If you're proposing an article about "smarter dieting" to a publication that targets women in their thirties, it's smart to mention that "according to Such and Such Big Study, 40 percent of all women between the ages of 29 and 39 are currently on a diet, and an additional 25 percent have dieted or plan to diet this year." This tells the editor that at least 65 percent of her readership will be interested in your article. If you want to really impress an editor, spell out what you know about her magazine's demographics: "Since 90 percent of your readers are homeowners, I believe an article about the pros and cons of refinancing a mortgage would be of great interest to them."

else is going to have to cover for you at the last minute. It's a big inconvenience when a writer doesn't come through, and no one wants to be responsible for hiring an unprofessional writer.

You have to be so irresistible and so convincingly professional that you override this editor's fear. And you have about 10 seconds to do that: the amount of time the editor will invest in your query.

In that 10 seconds, you must prove how well you know the magazine, and that your piece deserves a spot in it. You must do more than point out a new study. Even when pitching a short piece, you can gain an edge by packaging that new study with other studies or ideas. For example, let's say I read about a nutritional supplement that's been proven to decrease body fat. Well, fine, but why should an editor pay me to write about it when she can read that same study herself and assign it to someone she already knows and trusts?

So instead, I'm going to go searching around until I find not one, but four or five nutritional supplements that have proven positive effects on weight loss or body fat reduction, and I won't just read one study about each of them: I'll read several, to make sure my facts are reliable. Or I'm going to track down a person who has lost a lot of weight using that supplement. Or I'm going to look for the opposite: someone who will refute the claims in that study. Or I'll interview the person who discovered the weight loss properties of that supplement in the first place and find out if there's an interesting story behind it. Doing these things shows the editor that I know how to think, not just regurgitate—and it makes me more valuable.

So, let's say I'm that writer who wants to do "the skinny on the strawberry" for *Self*. I'm not going to read a couple of articles about the nutritional value of strawberries and then pitch it to Nicci. I'm going to talk to scientists, farmers, and nutritionists to ask if they know anything *new* about strawberries. I'm going to check out the vitamins and antioxidants in strawberries, then research those.

For example, I can easily find out that strawberries contain folate—then I can do thirty seconds of research on PubMed.com and find a brand new study that says high folate intake cuts former smokers' risk of lung cancer almost in half, and I can cross-reference this by talking to people at lung cancer associations and other cancer researchers. Or I could research what happens to strawberries' nutritional value when they're boiled and canned (for jams and jellies), dried (for cereal), or used in juice, yogurt, pies, etc. Are they still as good for us as when they're fresh and whole?

This is part of my market analysis: learning how deeply to dig for different markets. If I were going to pitch a story about strawberries for a short article in a pregnancy magazine, I might just need one main study: one that shows that folate intake reduces the risk of birth defects. Chances are that the pregnancy magazine hasn't already done twelve articles about strawberries in the past six years, so I might not need to go too crazy on my pre-pitch research. But a simple analysis of *Self* and other health and nutrition magazines should teach me that the more a magazine has discussed my topic, the deeper I'll have to dig to find a reason for them to throw it into the editorial mix again.

By the way, six seconds after I thought of that, I sold *ePregnancy* a filler about strawberries. It pays to brainstorm!

Tone, Style, and Format

Notice the style and tone of articles in magazines for which you'd like to write. For *Family Circle*, aside from the humor page, most of the articles are straight-forward—not irreverent, sarcastic, or overly-sentimental. Contrast that with *Jane* magazine: the whole magazine is humorous, irreverent, and very sarcastic.

Look at the way *Family Circle* handles heartwarming material in contrast to the way *Woman's World* handles it. *Woman's World's* articles tell stories in "scenes," bringing readers through the story as if they were watching a movie or reading a very short novel. *Woman's World* wants writing that uses strong emotion, as well as dialogue and sensory description. And lots of weeping (yes, I am bitter. I wrote a story for *Woman's World* and they added three weeping incidents without my consent). They also have a very specific "formula" for the openings of profiles: They start with a climactic moment in the story, then go backwards and tell the story chronologically. *Woman's World's* reading level is also lower than *Family Circle's*.

Let the Readers Lead

If you really want a leg-up on your competition, you can even check to see if the magazine has an online message board. If so, go there and see what people are talking about. See which articles they're reacting to. See what kinds of questions they're asking. Then prepare to tell the editor what you found and how you can interest these readers.

When I checked Budget Living's *message board today, I found that two readers were asking for suggestions for throwing a creative baby shower, and one was asking for ideas for a bridal shower. Several readers responded with creative ideas, which shows that this topic interested them, too. Now I can jot down this information to remind me to tell the editor that their readers want to know how to throw great showers, and that I have a wealth of ideas for them.*

Now read the editor's note in the beginning of the magazine, and see what kind of information you can glean. The editor will often give clues as to which were her favorite articles, or the kind of reaction the magazine received to a past article. Take note, too, of which articles are mentioned in the "Letters to the Editor" section. Controversial is fine—even if you see letters that seem to cast an article in a negative light, it means that the audience read the article and cared enough to respond to it!

You can bet that any writer who stirs up readers enough to invoke lots of mail, whether it's positive or negative, will be hired again (provided, of course, that the mail doesn't say that the writer's facts were all wrong), and a topic that generates lots of mail will likely be repeated. Negative mail about an article will often spark the editor's desire for a "rebuttal article." (For example, if an article about the dangers of living together before marriage got a lot of heat, an editor will be eager to assign an article about why it may be better to test the waters before saying "I do.")

Now check out the article formats of the magazines that are the likely candidates for your writing. For now, you want to get very familiar with just a few magazines, and probably just a few sections within those few magazines. (It's almost impossible to do a deep study of a hundred magazines at once.)

If I've made it a goal to break into the "Life Lessons" section of *Shape* magazine, I'll want to see how the articles are structured, so I flip on over to this section and see "Achieve Your Dreams" in the October issue. There's a deck, then a lead: A 36-year old woman decided to open a café, even though her family and friends told her she was crazy to try. Her story is told and wrapped up in two paragraphs: She opened the café, it's very successful, and her loved ones are sheepish. Then there are three paragraphs that tell readers why they just read that story: because they're about to learn why they, too, should set high goals and quit playing it safe. Included here is a quote from the author of a relevant book. The rest of the article is in list format: six tips for how to achieve major life goals, addressing the reader in second-person ("you"). Anecdotes and quotations from a psychologist are sprinkled throughout. There is no wrap-up paragraph at the end.

Now I'll look at this same section in the November issue and I'll find the article "Make a Major Life Change." Sure, it would make my life easy if this article was structured exactly the same, but it's not. This one contains a deck, then a tiny introductory paragraph that tells readers what they're about to read: an article that helps them figure out if they're ready to make a major change in their lives. Then there are four subheads, each describing a symptom that suggests the reader is ready for a change. Each subhead is followed by a long-ish paragraph or two explaining what the symptom means and why it's relevant.

Again, there are many quotes from a couple of psychologists and life coaches, and the article addresses the reader in second person.

What can you glean from this? First, you may have success with a list article. Even though the second article I analyzed isn't a numbered list, it could easily have been so: "4 Signs That You're Ready For a Major Life Change." If your article won't be a list, know that you will at least need to divide it up with subheads. Second, know that you'll need to address the reader in second-person, use a straightforward tone, find some mental health professionals to quote, and perhaps find an anecdote or two to include (but not more than that; the articles are primarily advice-driven, not story-driven). Aside from the introductory paragraphs, the rest of the paragraphs tend to be long, and you can skip the "summary" at the end. So, while there is no cookie-cutter format here, there are common denominators you should notice.

Editor Stephanie Abarbanel suggests that writers study how *Woman's Day*'s format differs from competing magazines like *Good Housekeeping* and *Redbook*. If you can reproduce her format, she says she'll pay attention.

Store all this information deep in your brain, on index cards, or in your notebook, for future reference. When your family bugs you for spending so much time on the couch, wading through magazines, remind them you're researching. Allow yourself the time you need to study your craft before rushing out a thousand copies of your first article to every editor on the planet.

Other Clues to Use

Once you've devoured the magazine and ascertained which sections and departments are open to freelancers, the tone and style of the magazine, and which articles got a strong response, it's time to study the magazine's demographics.

In the case of *Family Circle*, it's fairly obvious that the magazine is geared toward mothers; there were many "parenthood" articles, and, after all, the title is *Family Circle*. But in case you weren't sure, check out the advertisements. Take a look at the ads and notice who's buying space in the magazine. In this case, I find ads for toilet paper, milk, shampoo, cereal, and stain cleaner—all "mom-focused" ads. But let's go a step further and try to figure out what *kind* of moms we're targeting. These aren't ads for luxury cars or expensive products; they're ads for everyday items you'd find in the grocery store. So you can assume the magazine is for practical moms who are probably not rich.

Then study the media kit for further information. A media kit is designed for advertisers, but it's a wonderfully useful tool for freelancers, too. In it, you can find information about who reads the magazine (age, sex, income, marital status, location, etc.), what the magazine's focus is, the magazine's circulation and frequency, and sometimes editorial tidbits such as subjects they frequently cover, best-loved columns and features, and editorial plans for the future.

In *Family Circle*'s case (as is the case with most magazines nowadays), the media kit is online; you'll find it at www.familycircle.com/info/adinfo.jsp. There, we discover that the median age of their subscribers is 48.6, so this group of readers is likely to have teenage and even adult children, although *Family Circle* does feature articles about younger children.

A little more than half of readers went to college, 62.1 percent are married, and their median household income is $52,959. By age 48.6, most of these married readers aren't looking for articles about how to survive the first year of marriage, or how to adjust to family life. But they may very well be interested in articles about how to keep a romance alive or how to claim time for themselves in the midst of family responsibilities.

Finally, almost 80 percent own a home, and 58.6 percent are employed. So they may be interested in articles about getting ahead in the workplace, paying off a mortgage, or keeping household bills down.

Always read the magazine's mission statement to glean more information about tone and content: "As America's family answer book, *Family Circle* has, for the past 71 years, provided women with timely, important, reliable and relevant information and advice on family, food, home, health, finance, beauty, and fashion. Always realistic, attainable, and affordable, the information found in *Family Circle* energizes and empowers readers . . . and the result is unparalleled response to the editorial and advertising alike."

From this paragraph alone, you can see which subjects are most important to editors, and the tone of the magazine: "realistic, attainable, and affordable" would not pertain to a magazine like *Robb Report*, which is all about affluence and luxurious living. *Robb Report*'s mission statement is nearly the polar opposite: "*Robb Report* magazines and web sites are exclusive guides to living for high net-worth individuals who have a passion for celebrating life and success. *Robb Report* speaks directly to this elite audience of affluent, discerning consumers through engaging, dynamic editorial that explores, with authority, the most unique and exciting experiences the world offers."

A quick look at their media kit shows us how their readers differ from those reading *Family Circle*: To start, their readers' average household income is more than a million dollars a year! These people are probably not looking for decorating tips (they have interior decorators for that), tips for getting their homes organized (they have maids), or tips for storing leftovers—but *Family Circle*'s readers might.

If you can get your hands on a magazine's editorial calendar, all the better. It is generally included in a magazine's media kit, and often found on the magazine's web site. If you don't want to spend a lot of time hunting around, consider a subscription to Wooden Horse's media directory at www.woodenhorsepub.com, which contains editorial calendars and demographics for more than 2,000 magazines in the U.S. and Canada.

Editors often schedule special sections and "themed" issues based on what an advertiser is planning to push during a particular month or season. Most won't admit that publicly, of course; in fact, many editors talk about the "separation between church and state" at their magazines (editorial being the church, sales department being the state). But do you think *Some Big Travel Magazine* just happened to time their "Four Wheelin' Adventures" article with the glossy spread from Big Truck Manufacturer? Of course, it does work in reverse, too—sometimes advertisers will specifically promote a certain product because they know a magazine is planning an issue with a relevant section or article.

"Our editorial meetings were partially driven by the advertising division," says Moira Allen, former editor of *Dog Fancy* and author of *Starting Your Career as a Freelance Writer*. "We would plan, say, a Christmas issue that would include articles encouraging readers to buy Christmas toys and gifts for their pets, or other pet-related products. Our advertising arm always wanted to make sure that we included seasonal care articles that would focus on seasonal products (such as sweaters and boots for dogs in the fall and winter). Once we came up with what we were going to cover over the next six months, that list went to the advertising department so they could target advertisers to go with our content."

Editorial calendars are the blueprints for future issues of publications: they outline any themes, topics, special inserts, etc. that are planned to appear in upcoming issues. If you know well in advance that a particular issue will feature certain themes or topics (based on advertising, holidays, or otherwise), you can plan your query in advance and release it just as the editor is beginning to make assignments for the issue.

Because lead times (the time between when an article is accepted and when it appears in the magazine) vary widely, check the market's guidelines to estimate when to query. If a market lists a lead time of three months, you can estimate that you'll need to query about five months in advance. (Leave two months for an editor to read your query and assign it, time for you to write it, and a possible rewrite by you or the editor.) Some require longer leads, and some (especially online markets) have practically no lead time at all. I've often submitted an article to a web-based market and seen it appear on the web site within days.

By the time you've done all that homework, you should have a very good idea of where your idea will, or will not, fit in the magazine, and when you need to submit it.

Finding Ideas and Sources for Departments

If you let your market be your guide, then you probably didn't come up with a Big Idea first. Rather you waited until you studied the magazine first, and then came up with an idea to suit it.

For example, maybe I read the "Women Who Make a Difference" column in *Family Circle*, and it made me think, "Hey! My neighbor Helen organizes an annual Dance-A-Thon to raise money for literacy programs."

Or maybe I'm not that lucky, and my neighbors aren't all that interesting. I can get other people to come up with the ideas for me.

Your first option is to ask your friends and family, of course. Tell them you want to write for this particular column and ask if they know any extraordinary volunteers. If that leads nowhere, it's time to surf the web.

Many web sites are dedicated to helping writers hook up with "experts," which comes in handy if you're looking for an expert to quote. But it becomes even more helpful when you use these web sites to help you find organizations that can feed you great story ideas.

At each of these sites, individuals and organizations have paid for the opportunity to have writers like you contact them, so you know they'll be eager to talk to you. Each of them wants publicity. Some are authors with books to sell, some are universities who pay for the opportunity to have their professors make the schools look good by association, some work for government agencies, some are researchers who want to spread the word about their discoveries, some are doctors who want to build up their reputation, some are nonprofit organizations that want to raise awareness about their cause; you'll find all sorts.

Sites to See

➤ *www.profnet.com: You can submit a general query to their database of experts, asking for stories or anecdotes they can relate that will fit the column you are targeting. People can then respond to you by email or phone, whichever you prefer.*

➤ *www.guestfinder.com: Search this database by topic or keyword.*

➤ *www.yearbook.com: Search the database, or download the PDF of their whole* Yearbook of Experts *for no charge.*

➤ *www.journalismnet.com/experts/us.htm: You can find links to many other directories—about half aimed at one specific topic (like business or legal) and half general expert sites.*

If I want to write for *Family Circle's* "Women Who Make a Difference" column, I might look for organizations related to volunteerism, and then contact those listed to ask if they know of any great stories about women who have made a difference in their communities. Or I'll submit a general query to Profnet's database that looks something like this:

> *Hello! I'm a freelance writer with credits from several national women's magazines. I'm looking for stories I can pitch to* Family Circle *for the "Women Who Make a Difference" column. These stories feature women volunteers who have done something extraordinary and unique in their communities, such as coordinating unusual and successful fundraisers or donating their special talents to little-known, worthy causes. Know of any such women? Drop me a line.*

With any luck, I'll get responses, and then I'll choose an idea. Now I'll recall the word count for the column (1,500) and get set to pitch my idea to the editor.

Which editor?

Read the masthead and figure out who you'd like to approach.

If you have a health-related article idea, you first want to find out if there is a health editor. If there is no health editor, and it's a feature article, see if there's a features editor or articles editor listed. If not, try a senior editor, or even a deputy editor. The managing editor is your second-to-last resort; she is in charge of the daily operations of the magazine and may or may not have anything to do with hiring freelancers. The editor-in-chief is your last resort. You don't want to pitch to the editor-in-chief unless there are no other editors listed. (At a very small magazine, there may well only be one editor the editor-in-chief. If so, it's fine to pitch her.) If you're pitching a department piece (especially for front-of-the-book items), check to see if there's an editor's name listed on top of the page.

"I edit the Step pages for *ePregnancy*," says Julia Rosien. "It says so on most online guidelines and on the masthead of the magazine. Some writers continue to pitch full-length articles to me, though. Doing that holds up the query until it's passed along to the appropriate editor—which then drags things out for that freelancer who's waiting for an answer."

Take the time to target the appropriate editor, not just the first email address you happen upon. Not all editors are generous enough to pass along your query to the right person. Even if the one you approach is willing to play middle-man for you, there's no reason to start on the wrong foot if the masthead information is clear and easily available.

ASSIGNMENT

 Try this exercise with a magazine you want to target. You will need two or three copies of the magazine. Go through each issue of the magazine and answer the following questions:

Which sections or columns are open to freelancers? _____

What are the topics most frequently covered in the magazine? _____

What are the word counts for the types of articles or columns I might like to write? _____

Are experts quoted? If so, what kinds of experts? _____

Are the articles written in third-person or first-person? _____

What's the style and tone of this magazine's articles? _____

Who advertises in this magazine? _____

What can I learn about the readers from these ads? _____

If a media kit is available, what are the important demographics? _____

What is this magazine's mission statement or slogan, and how can I write something to fit that statement? _____

Descriptions of columns or regular features that I might like to write for. _____
_____

Chapter 5
FOBS AND BOBS AND WELLS, OH MY!

Inside This Chapter

- **Breaking in with front-of-book pieces**
- **Personal essay pros and cons**

The Front-of-Book Market

Most consumer magazines are roughly divided into thirds. The first section is called the front-of-the-book (FOB), the middle is the feature well, and the last section is the back-of-the-book (BOB).

These sections are like a good meal: appetizer, then main course, then dessert.

In the FOB, you'll find short items. Generally, these fall under department headings. They are generally not heavily reported pieces; rather, they may be quick tips, interesting tidbits, reader-contributed stories, book and movie reviews, news-y items, profiles, and so on, along with plenty of ads. Typically, this section is lighter in tone than the rest of the magazine.

The feature well includes the longer, in-depth stories that are generally on the cover. In most consumer magazines, these are the service and investigative pieces and celebrity interviews. In some magazines, there isn't any advertising in this section.

The BOB contains shorter items again, and often includes personal essays and commentary, along with the "continueds" of the feature articles and information about where to get products that are mentioned in the articles or shown in photos.

When I asked top editors where freelancers had the best shot of breaking into their magazines, almost without fail, they mentioned the FOB sections.

Chandra Czape at *Ladies' Home Journal* says that if writers are pitching her "cold" (that is, she hasn't worked with them before or asked them to submit), their best chance to prove themselves is with the shorter, up-front pieces, particularly the "Life Stories" section.

Scott Freeman, executive editor of *Atlanta Magazine*, says he needs "'Our Town' pieces, which are 400-word items at the front of the book. We're always looking for good ideas in that section, and it's how we usually introduce new writers into the fold."

In *National Fisherman's* writers' guidelines, editor-in-chief Jerry Fraser writes, "The 'Around the Coasts' section in the front of the book is a new writer's best chance to break in."

The guidelines for Academy of Television Arts and Science's *emmy magazine* say, "Most departments are written by regular contributors, but newcomers can break into Labors of Love—500-word, front-of-the book profiles of TV people and

---

How Do You Know When You Have a FOB?

➤ *Think about your own interest levels. If you're a woman, might you be interested in reading two paragraphs about how to keep your lipstick from fading? Possibly. Would you want to read two pages about it? No. Judgment: It's a FOB.*

➤ *Think about its timeliness. If your idea is based on something in the news right now and might not still interest readers several months from now by the time your feature gets published, turn it into a FOB. These are more easily rearranged, so the editor may be able to squeeze it into the next issue. Plus, if public interest has waned a bit by the time the magazine is published, they're taking less of a risk by publishing only 200 words about it, rather than 2,000.*

➤ *Can you say everything interesting about this idea in just a few hundred words or less? Then do. Never try to stretch a small, high-impact idea into a long feature; that tends to water down its appeal.*

➤ *If the idea is based on one interesting study you read, and you can't think of ways to relate it to a larger picture, it could be a FOB in the making.*

➤ *If it sounds like something that might become the subject of a question in Trivial Pursuit or a future game show, it's probably a FOB.*

➤ *Decide how much explanation it truly needs. I can easily dash off a list of ten cures for the hiccups. Sure, I could give an explanation of why each one works, and a doctor's quotation about how hiccups happen, and an anecdote about my friend who hiccupped for a week straight until he tried grapefruit juice, but do the subway readers really want all that? If your "list article" is pretty self-explanatory, consider it a FOB.*

their passions." And *Out's* editors strongly urge writers to pitch for the FOB "Out Front" section before trying to land a bigger assignment.

FOBs are typically easier to write than features, and less research-heavy. While you might have to do six or seven interviews for a feature, you'll probably need to conduct only one or two for a short piece. And this is exactly why editors would rather take the chance of assigning one of these pieces to you before giving you a fat feature. They'll see if you can handle the writing, the research, and the deadline before trusting you with something more in-depth.

Also, you'll have less competition. When most new writers pitch magazines, they're thinking features. They want to write the big how-to articles and trend stories. They haven't checked out the departments that conveniently already exist, ripe for pitching.

Natural Health's FOB is called "News and Notes," and it tells the reader exactly what it covers: "Latest Research, Interviews, Product Reviews, Tips, & Trends." What does it contain? Five ways to cut 500 calories a day from your diet. The "standout health benefits" of different kinds of juices, in chart form. A caution against using too much echinacea. Why you need to wash out your water bottle before refilling it. Nearly all of these pieces mention just one expert or study. In *Stuff's* FOB, you'll find a profile of a man who trains bears, a blurb about the "sport" of pig diving, "useless facts" (silly trivia), and music reviews.

In his article "So You Want to Be a Freelance Travel Writer" in *Freelance Job News*, Tad Hulse writes, "Magazine editors try out freelancers on these minor-league pieces because they are a low-cost loss if the writer tanks the assignment. Or worst-case scenario, the editor can write it himself or herself. Best-case scenario for a freelancer is the editor likes how you handled the piece and keeps an open ear to your ideas for full-length stories. The next assignment could be a lengthier, more pivotal piece, with, perhaps, travel expenses included."

True, you won't get paid as much for these as you would for features, but they're also less time-consuming and great for writers with shorter attention spans.

"I know some writers would cringe hearing this and not want to be bothered with that small stuff, but I work with several great editors at top national magazines who are always in need of FOB material," says Jennifer Nelson, who writes for publications such as *Fitness*, *Woman's Day*, and *Self*. "FOBs are simple, easy to research, usually only require one interview, and they're a great source of income in between longer work. Also, some pubs pay $2 a word, so writing a 400-word FOB and snagging $800 for a few hours of work is not too shabby either."

Of course, there are some writers who hate doing FOBs. One top freelancer who'd rather stay anonymous says, "When you're dealing with the FOB stuff, you're dealing with editors who are associates; they're not very good. They don't know what they're doing. And the other part is, they want the work of a 1,200-word piece. They want you to cram it into 300 words and pay you $300 for it." On the day we spoke, she had just turned in a 300-word piece that quoted two experts; the editor wanted her to go back and interview four more sources for the article.

She says that these short pieces rarely go smoothly for her, except at one magazine where the work is a "piece of cake" and the editor has realistic expectations. My experiences have been different; she and I have written for different magazines and I have not encountered editors who expect too much in such a short space. If you find an editor who is too "needy," finish out your assignment and don't work with that editor again. However if you're just starting out, be willing to go above and beyond to get those all-important first clips.

The Essay Market

Back-of-books (BOBs) are also good spots for freelancers, but usually contain fewer articles and can be more competitive. For example, take the last page of *Smithsonian*, which is cleverly called "Last Page." It's a humor column, and it's open to freelancers. And pretty much every humor writer in the world is trying to get their words on it. (One writer calls it "journalistic Everest.")

Similarly, there are a slew of writers vying for the first-person essay slots featured in the *Family Circle* BOB.

First-person essays and op-eds have both good and bad points for freelancers. They require no experience whatsoever, meaning that you don't need to submit clips with your piece. You don't send a query for a first-person essay (unless a magazine or newspaper specifically asks for it, which is rare); rather, you send the whole piece, because so much of it depends on your writing style and how you handle the material that an editor can't get an idea of how your essay will turn out from a synopsis. So if you're starting out, essays aren't a bad idea.

But essays also present two problems: first, nearly every writer wants to write them. They require no research, and they feel more like creative writing, so your competition will be stiff. And second, they don't make great clips for other types of writing. If you're proposing a how-to feature article, an editor won't know if you can handle it if all he sees are personal essay clips.

Opinion pieces need to stay tightly focused on one topic, warns Todd Raphael, online editor of *Workforce Management* magazine. He says that his most common reason for rejecting an op-ed piece is that "they float all over the board. There might be one opinion to begin with, but then there are three or four different points. Not three or four things that back up the main point, but three or four different points."

Personal essays have their own challenges, too. Not everyone can pull them off, because it's hard to be objective enough about your own life experiences to decide if you have something interesting that relates to a mass audience.

Sometimes it's not the biggest experiences in our lives that make great essays; sometimes it's the little stuff. An essay about my dear, departed grandmother and what she meant to me would probably not sell, and yet, the *Christian Science Monitor* just ran an essay called, "The Catch of the Day Lurked Behind the Refrigerator" by Richard Sorenson, in which he describes how a home-grown orange fell behind his refrigerator and how he worked to rescue it from the "dust weasels."

Profound? No. Just an entertaining and interesting slice-of-life with tidbits that others can relate to, such as, "For 45 strenuous, red-faced seconds I tugged and pulled, but with no result. The utter lack of movement convinced me that the appliance had grown roots that extended hundreds of feet into the ground."

Who hasn't tried to move a heavy object and felt so useless that you decide it's not your fault?

Then Richard tells us about his neighbor, who walked into the house without knocking and decided to help out: "Sebastian applied himself to the citrus-rescue problem. His solution was to get his fishing pole. He loves to fish, and his solution to almost any problem, including the national debt, is to get his fishing pole."

Don't we all know a character like Sebastian? Those qualities—someone who'd walk right into your house without announcing it, or someone who's McGuyver-ish with the innovative solutions (usually involving duct tape), someone who's obsessed with fishing, or a neighbor who's always ready to help in a pinch—are recognizable. Even if we don't know someone who fits all of these qualities, chances are good that we can picture Sebastian, even with only the few lines of description Richard gives us. "Relatability" is an important trait of personal essays.

Here, too, is a great example of why queries just don't work for essays. Imagine if Richard wrote to the editor and said, "In this essay, I will cover how an orange got stuck behind my refrigerator and how my neighbor and I got it out of there and ate it." Does this sound worthy of printed space to you? Not until you see how amusingly the writer will cover it.

Beware, too, of trying to have a "moral of the story" in your essays. Yes, they should have satisfying conclusions, but just as the trend in children's books is to avoid beating the reader over the head with a "lesson," so it is with personal essays. They are not usually there to teach or preach. They are there to be entertaining or inspirational, provide a good read, and feel like an interesting conversation with a friend.

Happily for writers, there's an upward trend in the use of personal stories in major magazines these days. Perhaps editors have noticed the ridiculous popularity of the *Chicken Soup for the Soul* series, or recognized the need for more warm, personal, uplifting, and fun material during a tough time of war and

---

A Dream Invitation

Barbara A. Tyler, a freelancer, actually had a Family Circle *editor track her down to ask her to submit humor essays. "In November of 2000, I penned a piece that began with the now infamous words: 'Martha Stewart will not be dining with us this Thanksgiving,'" she says. "This was my November humor column for* Today's Woman *(my local women's glossy)."*

The column, which had appeared only in this Kentucky and southern Indiana free magazine for women, was so loved that it has become one of the most circulated humor columns on the Internet—if you haven't seen it yet, just do a Google search for Barbara's opening line. Turns out that one of the column's Indiana admirers was the sister of a senior editor at Family Circle.

"Within a week of publication, I got a call from my editor telling me that she had been contacted by Family Circle," *says Barbara. "They wanted me to write for them and would it be okay for her to give them my phone number? Duh!"*

The editor rejected her first submission, which Barbara had specifically written for Family Circle, *but published her second, which she had written just for her own enjoyment. She's now sold six essays to them. She says, "My big tip based on this experience: Don't turn up your nose at writing for the smaller markets. You never know who may be reading them."*

---

economic recession. Perhaps they've noticed how much reader feedback they receive on these personal stories, or seen how popular blogs (short for "web logs," which are usually online diaries or running personal commentaries) have become. Whatever the reason, if you can spin a good yarn, the market is ready for you.

Back to the Well

Now, all of the advice about writing FOBs and BOBs is not meant to stop you if you have a great feature idea. The truth is that I write a lot more features than department pieces, and have broken into major magazines with feature assignments right off the bat. But that becomes easier to do as your bio and clips get more impressive. If you are not very experienced, your best shot is to pitch a shorter piece first and work your way up. However, a great feature idea is a great feature idea, and you don't need to try to cram it into 500 words just because that'll make it fit somewhere convenient.

At the end of the day, all editors are looking for the same thing: fantastic articles to put in their magazine. Show them that you can provide one and your level of experience will be secondary.

Chapter 6

PITCHING LIKE A PRO VERSUS PITCHING LIKE A SCHMOE

Inside This Chapter

- **The basics of a great query letter**
  - **Creating the right lead**
  - **Supporting your premise**
  - **Showing your expertise**
    - **Clips and bios**
  - **SASEs and e-queries**

Out of the Starting Gates

On to the nitty-gritty of just what makes a great query letter different from a bad, mediocre, or sort-of-okay query letter.

Here are the components of an irresistible query:

➤ The salutation
➤ The hook
➤ The synopsis
➤ The offerings
➤ The qualifications
➤ The call to action

Sounds simple enough, right?

Formalities are important when you're contacting an editor for the first time. If you're sending your letter by mail, make sure you've followed proper "formal letter" protocol (remember the 5th grade?), which should look something like this:

Your Name

Your Address

City, State, Zip

Phone Number

Editor's Name

Publication

Address

City, State, Zip

Date

Dear Ms. Brown:

Note the colon. Colons are used in the salutations of formal letters. Commas are used in friendly letters. You can switch to a comma once you've landed the assignment!

When writing an email query, it's up to you whether or not to include the addresses at the top. I don't. A few writers do. It doesn't seem to make a difference. In an email query, you can simply start with the "Dear Ms. Brown."

You've probably heard this before, but let me stress again that it is imperative that you not only address your letter to a specific editor personally (not "Dear Editor" or "To Whom It May Concern"), but that you spell the last name correctly. It's a big pet peeve among editors when a writer doesn't take the time to check spelling; it signals that the writer may not be careful enough when writing the article, either. You'll find editors' names on mastheads and in guidelines.

If you're not sure whether the name is masculine or feminine, rather than using "Mr." or "Ms.," use the editor's full name ("Dear Pat Riley:").

The All-Important Opening
Your first sentence is the most important part of the entire equation. The first sentence has to pack a major wallop. It has to entice, interest, scintillate, amuse, shock, or thrill the editor enough to make him or her want to read on. Put

yourself in a busy section editor's shoes. Today, you have to make two assignments, edit two more, check up on a writer whose work is late, help a writer who is having trouble finding a key fact for his or her story, consult with the graphic designer about layout, meet with the editor-in-chief about the upcoming editorial calendar, send out two contracts, bother the people in accounting about a columnist's missing check, and sort through the roughly 120 queries that are sitting on your desk and in your inbox. Half of them will be full of misspellings, six pages long, in red font, totally inappropriate for your magazine, and include a tribute to the sender's great-aunt. The other half will be well-written and in good format.

So, now you're down to 60. How many of those 60 are relevant to your target audience? How many are interesting enough that you can remember what they were about once you've read the next 20 queries?

That's why you need a killer hook. That first sentence has to capture the editor so fully that it will stick in her mind even after she's sidetracked by 10 different tasks.

That's why your first sentence should never be anything like,

"I would like to submit an idea for your consideration," or "I am an avid reader of your magazine, and now I have an article for you."

Forget the small talk and asking permission. Go straight into the selling point of your story. And just what is the selling point of your story?

Well, why did you choose this idea? What's unique about it, or touching, or shocking? How can you encapsulate that in one to two sentences?

Simple: Pretend you have only five seconds to get your point across before your message self destructs. Basically, that's the truth. If you fail to capture the editor's attention in the first few seconds, she probably won't read on—if she does, it will be with a strike against you already in her mind.

Your hook may be an interesting fact, or a controversial idea, or a common problem that you can solve. You will have to back up your first statement later, so don't exaggerate, but boil it down to the single most-interesting point of your idea. Here are some fictitious examples of great hooks:

> **By the year 2020, seven out of ten college students will have an incurable sexually transmitted disease.**
>
> **A high school student in Philadelphia has already made more money this year than you or I will in our lifetimes.**
>
> **Sex cures cancer.**
>
> **Michelle Smith, a woman with cerebral palsy, is suing Billy Joel because she didn't get a good seat at his concert this May.**

If you could magically gain the skill to read people's minds and know when they were lying, would you want it?

Joe Smith doesn't want to be a priest anymore.

Why do all of these examples work? Read any one of them, and the next thought in your mind, if I've done my job, should be, "Why?" Or "How?" If nothing else was written in that letter, wouldn't you be curious as to why Joe doesn't want to be a priest anymore, or how this high school student made so much money? Any time that you raise a question like that in an editor's mind, you've just ensured that he or she will read on with interest.

Examples of bad hooks:

Mary Smith is a 10-year-old girl in Sayville, NY.

Everyone wants to know how to better communicate with his or her spouse.

The Sundown Festival is the biggest craft fair in America.

Businessman Mark Smith can teach your readers how to be better bosses.

Why don't these work? They're just statements. Even though there may be something interesting about them, you could easily read any of those sentences and walk away, never thirsting to know more. They don't raise the same questions in a reader's mind. They don't tease, they don't grab, and they don't give you a hook on which to hang the rest of your query.

Openings like the above are fine for school papers, but they're not fine for query letters. Your first sentence is meant to approximate the opening of your article. The editor has to know that you will be able to entice readers. What would make a reader stop to read your article, rather than flipping pages and skimming it? The same principle applies; you have to engage the reader in the first sentence. If you save your interesting stuff for later (afraid of giving it all away at once, maybe), you've done yourself a great disservice.

The rest of that first paragraph must "pay off" the hook, meaning that it must explain or expand a bit more on what you just wrote. If you made a shocking statement like, "Sex cures cancer," back it up in your next sentence: "Al Smith, a reputed cancer researcher from the Spiffy Institute in Alabama, came to this conclusion after comparing recovery rates of nuns versus prostitutes. Prostitutes had a 35 percent higher recovery rate, which led Smith to further investigate the possible link between their sexual behaviors and their cure."

Keep your first paragraph short and to the point, preferably no more than three to four sentences. Some hook sentences can stand alone. Take this one, for example, which could be sent to an e-zine:

How close are you sitting to your computer monitor right now?

If it's closer than 20 inches, doctors warn that you may be doing serious damage to your eyesight. Thanks to the growing numbers of young people who regularly use laptop computers, or sit too close to a desktop computer for several hours a day, many experts are concerned that this generation's youth will have the highest rates of vision impairment in United States history.

Notice how the first sentence stands alone? It has much more impact this way than if I had combined it with the second paragraph, because the way it stands, the reader is subconsciously being asked to pause. That pause allows the reader to think about the first sentence a little longer: "Hmm. How close *am* I sitting?"

Very short paragraphs (one to two sentences) are for emphasis. Using this technique sparingly through your query will help to highlight the parts to which you want the editor to pay particular attention.

Without realizing it, writers often lean on a few different "old standards" when searching for a good lead. Here are some of them:

The Zimmerman Lead

Most writers assume (and not altogether incorrectly) that they need a human touch to their articles. Therefore, they try to begin their articles and queries with the story of one person who represents the issue, problem, or point of the article. This person is meant to give a "face" to the facts and figures. It often works just fine, but examine your Zimmerman carefully before leaning on this technique.

A good Zimmerman may just be an everyday person, but there has to be something noteworthy about him or her.

Let's say you're writing an article about simple techniques for starting a vegetable garden, and you want a humanized angle. You might start like this:

Jan Smith walks through the aisles in the grocery store, sniffing and poking and inspecting the vegetables. She loves vegetables, but her budget is tight, and she can't stand the fact that every week, she winds up throwing away half of the produce she buys because it turns bad before her family uses it. If Jan only knew how easy it was to start her own garden, though, she could save money and only pick produce as she needed it.

What's wrong with that lead?

Primarily, who cares about Jan? What's so interesting about her? It's obvious that we're supposed to empathize with and relate to her, but why do we need her?

The general rules are this: If you're not going to return to your Zimmerman later, you don't need him or her. In this case, Jan isn't going to be a major part of your article. You won't be quoting her extensively or coming back to discuss her unique situation. You were only using her to get you started. Forget it.

Second, try the "who cares?" test. From an unbiased view, if you were reading this lead elsewhere, would you care enough to read an article that looks like it's going to be about Jan Smith?

To use one of my own Zimmermans as an example, see what you think of this:

> **Imagine living in a time and place in which a child could be turned away from necessary medical treatment and left to die because her I.Q. was too low. Imagine her parents' desperate pleas to save her life were ignored by doctors, surgeons, and the government. You wouldn't have to stretch your imagination too far; that time is now, and that place is everywhere in the world.**
>
> **Now give that imaginary child a name: Katie Atkinson. Katie is a nine-year-old girl with Down syndrome from South Yorkshire, England. An estimated 50 percent of people with Down syndrome have congenital heart defects, and more than one-third develop cardiac manifestations that lead to early death if left unrepaired. Katie needs a heart transplant to save her life, but British hospital policies dictate that she will not even be considered for the waiting list, let alone receive the needed operation.**

In this instance, although I've introduced her in the second paragraph, Katie was my Zimmerman. She was the thread that tied this article together. As I went on and described all of the policies, technical details, politics, statistics, etc. about transplants, I kept coming back to her story as the example of how all of this plays out in the "real world." I needed a Zimmerman for this piece to show how people in power can dictate policies that may look fine on paper, but fail to take into account the very real people whom the policies affect.

Her story is unique and compelling enough to carry the lead spot. Be sure that all of your Zimmermans pass the same test.

The Statistic Lead

Another common technique is to open with an interesting statistic or fact. Here are two examples:

> **There are at least 130 different kinds of parasites living in or on your body right now.**
>
> **The average SAT score in 1980 was 990. Today, it's 1050.**

Which one works, and which one flops?

I hope you chose the first one as the more effective lead. In this example, the forthright nature of the statement is much more useful than other alternatives, like "Scientists have discovered that there are a wide variety of parasites living peacefully in the human body."

The second fails because it's not shocking enough, provocative enough, or intriguing enough. The statistic would be fine later in the article—even later in the lead paragraph. But a stronger lead is needed. How about, "Are our children smarter than we are?"

Be especially wary of bogging down your reader with numbers or complicated facts right at the beginning of a piece. Let the reader settle into your subject matter, or the numbers will just detract from, rather than add to, the strength of your lead. One stat (if necessary) in the first paragraph is plenty.

Tie-ins

Writers often try to tie in their leads to events, holidays, or other news stories. This works only if the relationship between the two is obvious. When you're stretching to come up with a way to relate the two, or leaning on a larger or more publicized story to make yours seem "bigger," it's a definite sign that this lead isn't right for your piece.

For example, how many times have you seen this one?

> **While United States Presidential candidates George Bush and Al Gore were conducting national campaigns to outdo each other at the voting booth, eighth graders at Tralala Junior High School were listening to speeches from their own political candidates: Jimmy Doe and Sarah Brown, both vying for the position of student council president.**

Riding the coattails of an event that's obviously of much more significance rarely works. And it's too overdone. Your lead should be able to be interesting enough on its own; otherwise, it doesn't merit an article. Without leaning on the U.S. Presidential election, find something very interesting about the student council election that won't remind readers that your story is minor in comparison to the "real world" elections.

Ditto for pointless seasonal tie-ins:

> **'Tis the season to be jolly, but photographer Bob Johnson's holiday spirit was ruined when he found out an escaped cow had wandered into his store and eaten all of his film.**

Now, of course, if your story has an obvious tie-in, don't neglect it. If your story centers around a man in the community who has been playing "Santa Claus" at orphanages for 20 years, by all means, start with clever Christmas references.

Bad Puns

I run an online magazine for writers (whose name is a pun in itself, but that was mostly to get listed first alphabetically in search engines), so I see bad puns almost daily. A writer will propose an article about how to write something-or-other, and the lead or headline will be something along the lines of, "Joe Shmoe knows the write way to do it," or "Negotiating with editors is all write." Puns may feel clever when you're writing them, but they usually make editors groan—especially if it's likely the editor has seen that same play on words a hundred times before. Cuteness almost never appeals to editors.

Question Leads

Question leads can be very effective. They can also fall flat. It is often said that a lawyer never asks a witness a question if he or she doesn't already know the answer. The same has to go for the writer. If you're not absolutely confident that your editor (and your reader) will answer the question in their minds just the way that you intend them to, don't ask the question.

A good question lead:

> **How would you like to extend your life span by five healthy years just by receiving a simple injection?**

Who in his right mind would answer "no" to this question? It works because it's pretty obvious that almost all of your readers will care about this topic and will want to find out more about how this is possible.

A bad question lead:

> **How would you like to learn how to design web pages in just one afternoon?**

It's too easy for your editor and readers to just say "no" to this question. It's not a universal-enough topic; even if this goes to a market for beginning computer users, there's no guarantee that the majority of them will have any interest in learning how to design web sites. And there's no guarantee that the ones who are interested haven't already done something about it.

The "That's What" Lead

> **Kids today are overmedicated and understimulated. That's what child psychologist Rita Joseph said at a lecture in Dallas.**

Unnecessary words. Skip the "that's what" and just stick it in quotation marks or paraphrase it ("Child psychologist Rita Joseph thinks kids today are over-medicated and under-stimulated"). Better yet, try something like, "If child psychologist Rita Joseph is right, then we're feeding our kids' mouths too much and their brains too little . . . "

Working Title Lead

You can also include the working title of your article in your lead (or elsewhere in your query) if you think it's strong. (A "working title" means that it's subject to change. It's the title you're using while working on the article.) You won't have much control over the title the publication chooses to use, but if you've thought of a smart title, it can help the editor visualize your story. It serves a function similar to your hook: an even shorter, more to-the-point statement about what's so interesting about your article.

Keep the Editor Riveted

Now on to the body of your query.

Your next paragraph is the "meat and potatoes" of your article idea. You have the editor's attention; now keep it. What are the key points of your article? What's interesting about this idea? Very concisely, and in a straightforward manner, tell the editor what you plan to deliver in this article. What will you teach readers, how will you inspire them, how will you entertain them?

Go over the body as many times as possible, and ask others for feedback when you can, to make sure that (a) there are no unnecessary words, and (b) your writing clearly expresses the intent of your article. The synopsis must cover all the major "points" of the article, and must back up the leading paragraph, offering proof or explanation of any claims you made.

This doesn't mean that your letter must be dry; by all means, if you're passionate and enthusiastic about the idea, let that show! You can be colorful and emotional while still being concise and on-topic.

When Good Email Goes Bad

If you're including lists, you can do it "bullet-point-style," provided it's a snail mail query; if it's an email query, substitute asterisks for bullets. Never use bullet points, "em" dashes, or any other fancy characters if you're sending an email query, since different email programs won't always be compatible with yours, and may turn your symbols into nonsense characters.

When writing a query in Microsoft Word, the program will turn your straight quotation marks into curly ones by default, and some email programs will turn that into utter weirdness, which will look something like this on the other end: ¾I½m not going to the store today,¼ said Jerry.

Compose your queries in plain text format, or make sure all of the autoformatting features are turned off on Microsoft Word or other word processing programs.

What can you include in your synopsis? Great quotations, fascinating facts, examples, and a statement about the points you intend to make. Explain what the reader will take away from this article. Show why it's different from other articles on this topic.

You don't need to include all of these elements. Don't strain to find great quotations or statistics if you don't have them, or if they don't apply. In the end, it's your big idea that needs to speak for itself in this paragraph or two; you're simply the medium for conveying that idea. It's very transparent when a writer is desperate to unload an article. Suddenly, you'll see lots of phrases that sound suspiciously like a used car salesman's pitch: "groundbreaking," "biggest," "life-changing," "the best thing since sliced bread."

If your idea is good enough, you won't need to tell editors why they should buy it. It will be obvious by the strength of your synopsis.

Picture it this way: If a woman is beautiful, she doesn't need to say so. A woman who keeps announcing, "I'm hot. I'm gorgeous" doesn't make you believe it's so. In fact, you probably scrutinize her more carefully to find reasons to poke holes in her claim. But if that same woman were simply walking down the street with a confident smile, you might just think to yourself, "What a beautiful woman." So it is with your story idea: Let the beauty of it just walk down the street with a confident smile. Don't let it brag.

The synopsis may be one paragraph, or it may need to run two or three or more. Try to gauge this according to the length of the proposed article: If your topic is fairly simple, and you only expect to write a 500-word article, you certainly don't need a 300-word synopsis. If your topic is complicated, and you're leaving out important points just for the sake of keeping it short, allow yourself more leeway. But not much!

When I asked Melissa Walker, editor at *ELLEgirl*, what mistakes writers make in query letters, she said, "Queries have to be concise. If they're long-winded, editors will think you're a long-winded writer. Brevity is beauty in a query (and in an article, really). We're not all publishing sprawling *New Yorker* stuff: Mags are in the space-saving business, so go short."

How short? When Melissa herself sends query letters, she keeps the synopsis to a paragraph; "maybe two if it's a big feature pitch."

Similarly, Bob Boze Bell, publisher of *True West* magazine, says, "If a query letter goes more than one page, I get antsy and suspicious. I like it short and sweet. Get to the point."

Often, if an editor likes your basic idea, she will ask for more details before making the assignment. That's when it's appropriate to give a more-detailed outline of your article. In the meantime, always leave them wanting more.

I have discovered two major exceptions to the "short and sweet" rule:

national women's and health magazines. If you're proposing a feature article to a high-circulation women's or health magazine, write a more in-depth query. I learned this after querying *Good Housekeeping* and *Ladies' Home Journal*. Both asked me to expand on my one-page queries. *Woman's World* had researchers and editors call me to get more details before assigning my article. *Prevention* assigned me an article based on a two-page e-query. *Cosmopolitan* is currently interested in two of my one-and-a-half-page queries. And I know another author who had similar experiences with *Woman's Day, Family Circle,* and *Redbook*. (And one exception to the exception: *House Beautiful's* editor told me my two-page query was too long.)

These kinds of magazines are less likely to take a chance on an unknown writer unless they are virtually guaranteed that the writer is capable of delivering quality work. Therefore, they want more of an "audition" than a single-page query. They want to see that you've already done research. They want quotations, experts, facts, and other proof that you have this article under control. I've still never gone over a two-page query, though I know a writer who occasionally sells articles from three-page queries!

"If it's a profile pitch for a one- or two-page piece, get everything in there that I need to know about this woman in one or two paragraphs," says Chandra Czape, deputy articles editor at *Ladies' Home Journal* and founder and president of Ed2010.com, a networking group for young and aspiring magazine editors. "If it's going to be a 3,500-word feature, then I need to have two pages at least, sometimes more, with all the stats up front and all the experts you're going to use. You could also write your lead so I have a good idea of what the tone is."

This doesn't mean you can be verbose or take your time getting to the point just because you have extra elbow room; it means only that you have to be more in-depth. You must still write as tightly as possible.

See the "Queries That Sold" section in Appendix A for further examples of good article synopses.

I've Got it Covered

The next paragraph ("the offering") of your query is the one in which you show the editor how easy you're going to make his job.

You're going to do the whole job, you're going to give him a no-brainer about where the article belongs, you're going to handle the research with ease, and you're going to do it on time. The easier you can make the editor's job, the more likely that you'll be hired. Editors have to coordinate and handle so many different things in each issue that every extra service you can provide means one less thing for the editor to worry about. These services include sidebars;

photos or suggestions for visuals; proposed heads, decks, and coverlines; background research and source sheets set up for easy fact-checking; etc. If the publication is in print, but has a corresponding web site, you can offer two versions: a longer one for the print edition, and a shorter one full of links to relevant web sites for the web version.

You don't have to be a photographer to offer photos, unless you're dealing with a major magazine that hires its own photographers. You can ask your subjects for photos, you can purchase a decent camera and take a selection of photos on your own (amateur photos are generally good enough for all but the biggest markets), or you can hook up with a local photographer. Many successful freelancers have working partnerships with photographers; the writer pays the photographer most of the fee he or she gets from the publication for the photo, minus the writer's commission (whatever fee you agree upon). If the magazine will pay you $200 for the photo, you might pay the photographer $175 and keep a 15 percent commission.

You can also look up stock photography online. If the publication can't afford to hire photographers, the art department may use stock photography instead. Generally, these are royalty-free images that can be purchased cheaply; some are even free for commercial use. Become familiar with some of these sites so you can add this to your offering list if an editor wants it. One caveat: Don't insult a major magazine by offering to get stock photos for them.

Some writers also like to mention the time frame in which they can get the article done. In other words, they'll say things like, "I can have this article complete within 30 days of contract signing." I used to do this every now and then, but soon realized editors don't really care when you want to finish it—they'll tell you the deadline. You can negotiate it, but it's really not your place to suggest a deadline without knowing what the editor needs first. What if she thinks it's a great-sounding article, but she needs it in two weeks to fill a particular gap? She looks at your query and wonders if you can handle it, because you said you'd need 30 days. Suggesting a short time frame also gets writers in trouble: If you say

---

What's in Stock

You'll find stock photography at these sites:

- ➤ *www.corbis.com*
- ➤ *www.comstock.com*
- ➤ *www.arttoday.com*
- ➤ *www.cyberphoto.com*
- ➤ *www.gettyimages.com*

A checklist of what belongs in the offerings paragraph:

➤ *If you can get photos, mention it.*

➤ *If you've studied the magazine and know where your article belongs, you can propose a word count, or suggest the column/section in which your idea may best fit.*

➤ *Offer to supply suggestions for headlines, decks, and coverlines (optional).*

➤ *If you have an idea for a sidebar, describe it.*

➤ *If you have secured interviews, mention this.*

➤ *If this needs to run by a certain date, mention it. (This applies if you're proposing coverage of a timely event or news story.)*

you can have a certain article finished in two weeks, you risk coming across as inexperienced. The editor may look at the query, see that it's a complicated subject that will require several interviews, and doubt that you know what you're getting into.

Now the only time I'll mention a time frame is when it's an editor I've worked with before and I need more time than usual, or when I'm proposing something timely and want him to know I can write it quickly to get it into an upcoming issue. For example, while working on this book, I came up with some great story ideas. I didn't want to put off querying them for a long time, so I went ahead and sent a couple of queries to my editors, but I let them know that I'd need six weeks to finish the articles, as opposed to my usual three to four (because I had to finish the book project, too!).

In short, putting in a time frame is optional, but I advise against it in most cases.

About Me and Why I'm So Wonderful

Here comes the part that new writers hate: the bio. If you've never been published before, just don't say anything about it! Never, ever point out, "Though I've never been published . . . " or "I've enclosed some non-published writing samples." Keep quiet about it and an editor may not even notice. Soon enough, you'll have plenty to mention in this section. If you have professional credits in any writing realm, do include them. Don't worry if they're not in the same field (i.e., if you've written technical manuals, advertising copy, greeting cards, etc.). Rather than specifying, you can simply state your credits in a manner like this: "I have written for several companies, including AT&T, General Electric, and Blue Mountain Arts."

If you have any particular qualifications that make you the right writer for this article, definitely mention them. For example, if you're proposing a piece about education reform and you are a public school teacher, don't leave out that fact! Or if you're proposing a piece about a screenwriter, and you've worked in the film industry, or if you're proposing a piece about using humor to cure depression, and your father was a stand-up comedian, mention it. If you have no credits at all, but do have another qualification, your bio might look like this: "As a former tax attorney with Law Firm X, I have two decades of experience helping entrepreneurs find tax breaks and deductions they never knew they could take, and I am still in contact with many top experts in the field."

One of the many reasons that you should always do a good job for every editor you work with is that editors know other editors, and they actually talk to one another. If you do a good job, they'll likely bat your name around to other editors. In fact, Chandra Czape at *Ladies' Home Journal* says she often calls one of her friends (six of them are editors at women's magazines) to ask about writers. "One of my good friends is an editor at *Glamour*, and I'll call her and say, 'I just need somebody who can give me a really good science-based piece here. Tell me who I should have do it.'"

But it can work against you, too.

Watch what you write in your bio; if you messed up on your deadline or had an argument with an editor, it might be better to omit the credit, even if it's an impressive one. If an editor notices in your bio a magazine where she has an editor-friend, she might just check up on you. Chandra says, "I'll call up Cara at *Allure* and say, 'What do you think of this writer? She's been writing for you,' and she'll say, 'She's a pain in my ass!' Knowing that everyone can get along with Cara, I'll think, if Cara can't get along with her, maybe it's not worth it for me to."

Writers are built on their reputations, so remember that one temper flare-up could ruin your chances of writing for many different magazines. Do your cursing *after* you hang up the phone with an impossible-to-please editor. Finish out each job professionally and gracefully, even if you never plan to write for that magazine again.

Editors job-hop with fervor, and they are often friendly with one another. Putting a magazine in your bio leaves you open to scrutiny, so be sure that editors there will speak well of you. This should also discourage you from exaggerating your credits; if you put *Jane* magazine in your bio, and someone checks your reference, an editor at *Jane* might reply with, "Laura who? Never heard of her. She's not in my files. Oh, wait . . . yes, she wrote a letter to the editor that was published in 1999."

Some editors, like Stephanie Abarbanel at *Woman's Day*, refuse to talk about writers outside of their own publications. "I think it would be a terrible professional breach," she says.

Formatting Your Query

➤ *Query letters should be single-spaced, with one blank space in between paragraphs. No indenting.*

➤ *Use 10–12 point standard black fonts (like Times New Roman or Arial).*

➤ *If you can't afford to have letterhead printed, you can design your own letterhead on your computer. Keep it simple and make sure it's easy to read.*

➤ *Use white or off-white 8½-by-11-inch paper for markets in the United States. (A4 paper is the standard in many other countries.)*

Parting Words

Finally, state that you are enclosing clips or writing samples and give a simple call to action: "I look forward to your response," or "I look forward to hearing from you," or "Thanks for your consideration, and I look forward to speaking with you."

Your ending greeting can be "Regards," "Yours truly," "Sincerely," "Best regards," or whatever other formality makes you comfortable.

If you've e-queried, be sure to include your phone number and address below your name (if you didn't include it at the top). Many editors prefer to make assignments by phone, and they'll need your address handy when it comes to sending you a contract. Don't include your web site address unless it's strictly a professional-looking site. Don't let the editor see a web site that's mostly pictures of your dog, Sparky, and stories about last week's birthday party at Aunt Hilda's. If you have excellent-quality writing clips or samples on your web site, then do feel free to include the URL.

Get Clipped

Clips are photocopies of your articles as they have appeared in print. Clips may also be electronic if you're sending an e-query; you can point the editor to a few web sites where your work appears, or you can copy and paste "clips" into the body of the email, below your query (this is how I generally handle it). Do NOT send attachments unless the editor has already specified that this is okay. Many editors will delete attachments unread because of the risk of viruses, and many spam filters will toss them out before an editor even has the option of making that decision. I can't emphasize this point enough; I'm amazed by the number of writers who continue to ignore this advice and have their queries deleted because of it.

If you paste articles into emails or showcase them on your web site, list the name of the publication, month, and year in which it first appeared at the bottom of the article. If the clip is appropriate for the editor's publication and you've kept the rights, you can also add, "Reprint rights available."

Here is where the judgment call comes in: Only include clips from publications that are very professional. That means no high school paper, Epinions.com, freebie local paper with no proofreader on staff, or badly edited e-zine. If you're sending a nonfiction query, do not include samples of your poetry and short stories. It makes you look like an amateur. There are some very rare exceptions to this: If you wrote a fantastic article for your college paper, or a super piece in a not-so-super publication, your writing will probably overshadow the venue.

"I don't care where a clip is from. If it's a clip, that's great," said Rachel Clark, deputy editor of *Premiere*, at a mediabistro.com panel discussion in 2003. "If it's from a local newspaper, if it's from a small magazine, it's probably not that fancy—it doesn't matter. They always say, and it's a cliché but it's probably a cliché because it's true, writers write. And you may be the most brilliant writer in the world, but if you don't have a clip to show me I won't know that."

So, what to do if you have no professional clips?

You have a few options: You can write a great query and hope no one notices your lack of clips, you can write an article or essay on spec, approach a not-too-competitive magazine or newspaper and boldly ask for your first assignment, or write up some sample articles.

Query With No Clips

If you're dealing with a small publication that has a shortage of writers, you might just get away with not having any clips. Write up a stellar query and omit any reference to writing credits. You might want to play up other credentials: you're a former English teacher, or you hold a degree in a subject related to your query, or have personal experience with the subject or access to someone who does.

Write on Spec

Pick a likely candidate for your work and write the article as if an editor had assigned it to you. Follow the right word count, quote the right sorts of experts, etc. Again, I'd advise aiming for small to mid-sized markets, but you just never know: Kelly James-Enger made her very first sale by writing an article about how to survive in the workplace after giving your two weeks' notice and sending it to *Cosmopolitan*. She sold her next article on spec to *Bride's*. Yes, I hate her, too.

I'm sure there are a few other writers like Kelly out there, but of course, this is very, very rare. More often, you'll hear stories like Tina L. Miller's: Tina attended a seminar about how to make money online, but she quickly realized this was a scam when they wanted her to fork out money and wouldn't allow her to take any paperwork home to discuss it with her husband. She was so upset by the way other attendees were scammed that she decided to write an article about it for a Wisconsin daily newspaper. Although the business editor loved the story, it didn't make it through the legal department (the scammers would undoubtedly sue), but he wound up giving Tina regular assignments.

Ask for the Assignment

Dr. Patricia Ferguson of Redding, California made a gutsy move when she wrote to the editor of a nuclear technical journal and asked for an assignment. In her introduction letter, she told the editor who she was, why she wanted to write for his journal, why she was qualified, and her interest in freelance writing. "The fact that I hold a doctorate didn't hurt," she says, but she also emphasized to him that she was comfortable interviewing doctors and talking about research. And once she got that first assignment, she never missed a deadline and made sure her work wouldn't need much editing.

Other writers have walked into a newspaper's office and asked editors what they could cover, or met editors at writers' conferences or networking parties and walked away with their first assignments.

"It's very hard to say 'no' with a curt brush-off when a writer stops by in person, well after deadline," says *The Wiregrass Farmer* editor Ben Baker. "But come in at deadline and I'll cut the writer off quick."

How does a writer know when editors are on deadline? The information might be printed in the paper. If not, call.

"Ask the first person who answers the phone, 'When is your deadline?' Call back two hours after deadline and make an appointment to meet with the editor, or just stop by," says Ben.

If you do attend a conference or event where editors are present, be careful not to be too pushy. "Don't pitch editors at a cocktail night, just talk to them like a friend or new acquaintance," says Melissa Walker, freelancer for magazines like *Glamour* and *Marie Claire*. "Save the pitch for the next day—if they like you as a person, they'll pay attention to your pitch."

Writing Sample Articles

This one won't work in the major league, but can certainly get your foot in the door in the minors. To show an editor that you're a capable writer, enclose something that represents your work very well. If you have already written professional-caliber articles that have not been published yet, include them. If you haven't, now is the time. Write two "sample" articles that you can use for a variety of queries. If most of your queries will be in the health genre, write up two short articles dealing with health topics. Don't put in any less effort than if you were being paid to write them. Conduct interviews, do research, and let yourself be your best editor. These articles are your calling cards, so be sure they're the best representation of your work. Post them on your web site, or just enclose them with your first queries.

If you decide to submit them for publication somewhere, all the better. Community newspapers are usually vastly under-staffed and welcome contributions, so you may be able to sell (or donate) your sample articles. If this is an option, take it. Building up your clip file is important business. Get published wherever and whenever you can to start, and make sure to save copies of all of your work in a safe place. (Mine are stored in transparent sleeves in a photo album so they won't age quickly.)

Even experienced writers sometimes write samples when they want to break into a new type of market. You may have great clips in the computer field, but now you want to write about food. How will the editor know that you have the skills to write about food if all she sees are articles about computers?

Will Your Clips Pass Inspection?

Some editors aren't generous about the "I don't care where a clip comes from" thing. When I last queried *Cosmopolitan*, the news editor told me she'd hold onto my query until I could send her some more impressive clips. Mind you, I sent her clips from *Woman's World*, *American Profile*, and Salon.com, and an article I'd just finished writing for *Prevention*, but this wasn't good enough. She told me her executive editor had "pretty strict guidelines" about using writers who already had extensive experience with national magazines writing about the topic they wanted to write about for *Cosmo*.

She seemed apologetic about this, possibly because I had come to her on a recommendation from one of their regular freelancers, but it seemed her hands were tied, at least for the moment. I promised to send her more clips on the topic as soon as I had them, but it felt awfully silly to me. Why wait until I've already written about the topic for another national magazine?

On the other hand, some editors aren't strict about whether or not you've published on that particular topic or for their particular audience before, but they do want to see that you've worked for recognizable, respectable publications.

"I'm an editor at a magazine that reaches 14 million people," says Chandra Czape of *Ladies' Home Journal*. "I'm not going to publish the woman who's never had anything published before. We're looking for a more seasoned writer."

Although she prefers that writers have clips from major magazines, she won't ignore clips from trade journals or newspapers.

And diversity isn't always the way to her heart. "There are the people who have so many magazine clips from everywhere, and you start to realize the reason they write everywhere is because nobody wants to hire them twice. You see one clip from every magazine they've ever worked at, and you think, 'Hmm. Why is it that they can't work at the same place more than once?'"

Indeed, some experienced writers have learned to coast on their bios. Once they've had some major assignments under their belt, they get cocky and sloppy because it becomes easy for them to break in at other magazines. A possible way to assuage an editor's fears that you may be one of these writers is to include two clips from the same publication, or to note in your query that you regularly freelance for certain publications.

Some editors also pay attention to the dates on your clips.

"People send me clippings from, like, 1981," says Stephanie Abarbanel of *Woman's Day*. "Don't do that. If you don't have anything in the past two years, don't send them. It makes you look so bad."

So, what to do if your best clips are more than two years old? Chop off the date. When pasting the article into an email, just leave out the publication date. When sending by postal mail, cut off the date before photocopying if possible. One of my favorite clips is three years old, and I still use it—but I also include a more recent clip or two, which shows editors that I haven't gone three years without an assignment.

These are not things to worry about if you're querying *True West* magazine. Publisher Bob Boze Bell admits that he rarely reads clips. "I just glance to see if there's anything I like and then I go see what it is they want to write for us," he says. "We really don't care about a writer's past. We're looking for new talent we can use and abuse until they get so big they don't need us anymore."

To SASE or Not to SASE

If you've read this far, you already know that I advise you to query by email whenever possible. But if that's impossible, or if you don't get responses to your e-queries to certain publications, suck it up and start sticking those stamps.

Sending SASEs (self-addressed stamped envelopes) is a sort of self-deprecating act. Except in the greeting card market, I don't think I've ever gotten an acceptance letter by the U.S. mail. No, when I see an envelope with my handwriting on it, it's bad news. The truth is that if an editor is going to assign something to you, he'll do it by phone or email.

However, if you don't enclose an SASE, you get to stay in Limbo Land for months, wondering if your query has been tossed or is still under consideration. Almost no editor (in the magazine world or the book world) will return your material or send a rejection without a SASE. It's up to you if you can handle that, but I prefer a response, especially so I know whether to move on to my B-list markets. (If all of my A-list markets have turned down the query, it's time for me to come up with some new possible markets for it. But it would be a shame to get an acceptance from a B-lister and then find out an A-lister actually wanted it.)

Fold your SASE in half or thirds; don't try to find smaller envelopes that fit within your original envelope, or the editor will have to play origami to figure out how to send your response.

When querying publications in other countries, you must include an International Reply Coupon (IRC) instead of a SASE. These are available at the post office.

Be aware that about 30 percent of all markets will never bother sending back your SASE. It's annoying, but unavoidable. My general rule is that if a publication has had my snail-mail query for more than two weeks beyond its stated response time and I don't have an email address I can use to check in, I assume it means "no" and move on. Occasionally, if it's a publication that's very important to me, I will send a follow-up note to make sure they received the letter. Otherwise, I simply forget about them, and I advise you to do the same. You have better ways to spend your time than to beg impolite editors for answers.

And there you have it—all the components of an irresistible pitch.

Chapter 7
STYLE AND CHUTZPAH

Inside This Chapter

- **Trying on different query styles**
- **Overcoming fear of rejection**
- **Tracking your goals**

Your Query Style

Just as most writers develop a signature style in their articles, you'll also develop your own query style over time.

Rather than starting anew each time, wondering how in the world you're going to start, structure, or end your query, you will undoubtedly come up with little "tricks" and techniques that feel comfortable to you. This will save you time, mental energy, and will most likely help you make sales.

Figure out where your strengths lie. Do you come up with great, memorable titles for your articles? Use that to your advantage. One writer I know always introduces his queries with the proposed title centered and in bold, like this:

> **Dear Ms. Smith:**
>
> **I am writing to propose a lighthearted service article for your home and garden section.**
>
>

The REAL Garden Bandits
>
>
> **The worst garden bandits of all are far more insidious than slugs, aphids, squirrels, birds, or even moles. They're sneakier, bigger, and have been known to play on our emotions to trick us into allowing them to ravish our hard-earned, flourishing gardens.**
>
> **They're humans!**
>
> **These bandits may come in the form of a neighbor, cousin, friend, or family member. They sneak attack, showing up with compliments and "oohs" and "ahhs" to inflate our gardening egos.**

By the time they leave, however, the garden is mysteriously barren; completely stripped bare of its bounty. How does this happen?

➤ The problem

Most often, the cause of this frustrating situation is generosity. Garden bandits twist words and take advantage of any invitation of admittance. Look inward; did you say, "We have more tomatoes than we could ever use—please take some?" Come on, admit it. You did. However, your vision of "some" and your bandit's vision of "some" are likely very different. Bandits often define "some" as "all except the rotting and withered ones."

➤ The solution

There are several steps to follow to ensure bandits don't strike you when you're most vulnerable—at harvest time. The article will include several tips, such as:

When a bandit steps near your garden, be sure you're the one in control of the container he or she will use to transport out your goodies. Don't hand over a shopping bag; offer up a disposable Tupperware or a large sandwich bag instead.

If you know the bandit is coming, do the picking yourself, before-hand. Put the fruits of your labor into a container in the refrigerator or on the counter, and hand it over as soon as the bandit walks in, to avoid any confusion.

If the bandit asks for more, explain that you have promised some to your [neighbor, favorite aunt, grandmother, best friend, doctor], and need to reserve the rest.

If the problem becomes chronic, you may wish to erect a small sign by the entrance of your garden: "Come enjoy our garden's gold, but please don't take more than you can hold," or "We hope our garden brings you pleasure, but please leave us some of its treasure!"

I would love to share this article with your readers. I am a full-time writer with hundreds of national and online credits, recently including *Woman's World, Woman's Own, Writer's Digest,* and Salon.com. Two clips of my writing are enclosed. I look forward to your response.

Regards,

Jenna Glatzer

Yep, that's one of my actual queries, and yes, I stole my friend's technique (and broke my rule about not starting out with an "I'm writing to propose . . . " type of sentence, because beginning the letter with the title seemed awkward to me). I included the whole query to point out another stylistic choice: bullets.

Some writers find it very natural to incorporate bulleted points or numbered lists in their queries to emphasize the structure of the proposed article. This is best used in moderation (in other words, don't let your entire query become a whole page of 18 bulleted points). It can be very effective if your idea lends itself to this style. For example, if your proposed article is "10 Ways To Save Money At The Grocery Store," it may be very smart of you to write a short explanation of three or four of those techniques. Instead of writing them in paragraph form, it seems a more obvious choice to write them as a denoted list.

These kinds of techniques (the centered headline and the bullets) also add visual appeal to your query without losing professionalism. Since you can't express yourself with colorful stationery or cute graphics without making an editor cringe, if you can think of a legitimate way to make your words more visually appealing, all the better.

Another writer I know starts every lead with two actions and a description, like this:

> **Handing out cigars to everyone in sight and showing both rows of his pearly whites, Ken McAffee is the quintessential proud new father.**

Or this:

> **Gears grinding and thin paint chipping off, the old Jeep Cherokee sputters its way down the hill.**

This system becomes a shortcut for him, both in his queries and in his articles. It saves him time in trying to brainstorm new leads, because he knows the components he wants to use.

You may find similar shortcuts that come naturally to you. For example, you may start with a complicated thought, followed by a simple thought, like this:

> **Joe Smith is a culinary preparatory artist, specializing in root vegetables that require precise timing and freshness. That is, he's a fry cook at McDonald's.**

Or the reverse.

> **Meditation can make you smarter. Guided meditations such as the Brain Sync series use specially tuned sound waves layered underneath soothing music to quickly ease your brain into the theta state, the state in which you are most receptive to learning.**

You may find that you like to end your queries with a cliffhanger or other kind of tease that leaves the editor dying to know how the article will end, such as:

> **Unfortunately, this woman who had dedicated most of her life to researching the cure for cancer soon found herself praying that chemotherapy would keep her alive long enough to finish her studies.**

> **Would you like to hear the rest of her story? I'd love to share it with your readers in an 800-word profile.**

Now, chances are, the editor isn't going to assign this article to you without knowing the "rest of the story"—but if she wants to know what happens, she's going to have to call you, which increases your odds of getting the contract about a zillion percent.

Some writers are most comfortable starting with strong statistics or shocking facts. Others like to start with a powerful quotation, such as:

> **"I knew my work was helping to kill people, but I couldn't afford to stop," says Ed Fleisher, a former copywriter for a major tobacco company.**

Hypothetical questions and statements may also become part of your query arsenal. For example:

> **What would you do if you knew you only had two weeks left to live?**

Or:

> **If Martians landed in Los Angeles tomorrow, they might be able to clear up the dispute between screenwriter Joe Wycland and director Karen Riant. The two have delayed the shoot of MY MARTIAN FATHER by six weeks already because they can't come to an agreement about whether Martians should have two or three eyes.**

Writers used to writing fiction may find that more descriptive, sensory passages work well for them. This kind of opening works very well for more "literary" publications. Here's an example I used to start a first-person essay:

> **Whether she fancies crinoline and lace-trimmed ankle socks or overalls and skinned knees, nearly every little girl the world over dreams of being a princess.**

> **Still dizzy from the endorphin rush that Goofy provided when he asked me to dance in one of the food courts, I had recently returned from my first trip to Disney World. No longer was my**

teenage baby-sitter the woman I aspired to be; now I had loftier goals. I was going to be Cinderella. Too precious to set her feet on the concrete and socialize with the ice cream-stained masses, she retained her mystique by dressing to the nines and sitting in her exquisite castle, waving that "royalty wave" to passersby.

You may also find that your style fits well with specific publications. While working on an assignment for Match.com, I learned that they prefer humorous, short articles that walk the line between "keeping it real" and maintaining a positive attitude about online dating. So, even though I could make fun of the differences between men and women, I couldn't be so insulting that I turned people off from wanting to meet a mate. In other words, I could make fun of the way men tend to "forget" to pick their clothes up of the floor, or the way women tend to cry at sappy movies, but I couldn't write about "those lying, cheating, slobby men" or those "weepy, nagging, jealous women." Because my writing naturally fit this style, I ended up getting regular assignments from this web site.

When you figure out these kinds of tips, either by studying the publication, or through guidelines and assignments, work them into your query style. If I query *Woman's World* again, I will be sure to mimic their formula in my letter: The lead will be a climactic moment filled with emotion and dialogue, and the rest of the summary will be a chronological—albeit abridged—version of the story.

Similarly, when I queried *House Beautiful*, the editor told me she wanted my article to be "more literary and poetic" than my pitch. Even though her response was positive, she was subtly telling me what I did wrong. I knew that next time, I'd better write a more literary and poetic pitch!

The editor of *Link* magazine once sent back an article of mine for a rewrite, explaining that they preferred a more "smart-ass" tone—intelligent, but edgy and funny. Again, I made sure to incorporate that into my next query, which was much more informal and fun.

Every once in a while, even after you've found a particular style that suits you, don't be afraid to break the mold. Routines can get very . . . routine. You

---

Other Techniques to Try
- ➤ *Metaphors and similes: Comparing giving someone a hickey to a dog marking his territory.*
- ➤ *Humor: Starting off your query with a joke or amusing anecdote.*
- ➤ *Alliteration: Headlines or email subjects that repeat the same beginning letter can catch attention, such as "Seven Simple Start-ups" or "Why Work the Web?"*

Before and After

Here's a section of the article I originally sent to **Link:**

Net One, an Internet Service Provider, is run by Charles Strader, Richard Skelton, and Pablo Mondal. The three met in the freshmen dorms, then moved into an apartment together. Opportunity knocked when Strader, who worked for the university's computer center, took a phone call from the owner of a hair salon. She sought help designing a web site; Strader volunteered, and Net One was born.

Here's what that same section looked like when I rewrote it:

Picture this: It's your sophomore year at Boston University. You and two of your closest college buddies are putzing around, trying to decide what to do tonight. You suggest a bar tour. Friend 1 wants to start a paintball fight with the guys down the hall. Friend 2 says, "Let's start our own web design and consulting firm." You squint and nod, realizing you can always do the first two activities tomorrow. You trek to the patent office, fill out the 834 required forms in triplicate, and rake in your first cool million the next morning.

Okay, so the "cool million" thing was a lie. But the rest of it really happened to Charles Strader, Richard Skelton, and Pablo Mondal, who comprise the successful-enough-to-merit-a-company-car-and-amazing-office-with-bay-windows business, Net One.

---

may find that what worked for you last year has now become stale. You may get bored with your own pitches, and therefore feel less ambitious about writing and marketing them.

So, if your style is generally shocking and informal, create a whole new persona for yourself and write a query that's subtle and classy. Just because you're usually a humor writer doesn't mean you have to pigeonhole yourself into that arena exclusively. Surprise yourself and write a terrific pitch to a health magazine. Or vice versa; if you write mostly heavily researched pieces, give yourself a mental break and work on a light-hearted, first-person parenting essay.

Chutzpah and Submissions

When I started teaching an online course about writing query letters, one of the things that surprised me most was that, even after writing, rewriting, and passing my "inspection," my students were afraid to send out those queries. Or they sent them off to one publication, got rejected, and gave up. Why in the world was this happening? They were afraid, plain and simple.

They were afraid they might be rejected. Afraid they weren't qualified enough yet. Afraid that an editor was going to show their letters around the office so everyone could laugh. Afraid their ideas weren't good enough. Afraid they might (God forbid) get an acceptance, and then not know what to do next. Afraid if they succeeded, they'd feel like impostors.

My first instinct was to say, "Buck up, little campers! Just send them out and quit thinking so much!" But my second thought was, "But *why* do these writers feel this way?"

Fear of rejection is obviously something everyone feels to some extent. Maybe you were humiliated at a junior high school dance somewhere, or turned down for a sports team, or had some foolish professor insult your best work. Experiences like this interrupt writers' ability to share freely. They inhibit writers' creative impulses, and make them second-guess themselves, wondering if they're really good enough, ready enough, smart enough. They're not worthless experiences; after all, if you had no fear of rejection, you'd be apt to submit the first piece of garbage that popped into your head. And re-submit all over the place, without fear of damage to your reputation.

It becomes a problem, however, when this fear paralyzes a writer and stops his potential career in its tracks.

Sure, you can sit there and worry about how editors will feel about you until the cows come home. Then you will guarantee that no one will laugh at you, reject you cruelly, send you a form letter, or ignore you completely. However, you will also guarantee that your work will never be published. And you don't really want that. I know you don't, or you wouldn't have picked up this book.

There's also the fear of moving up the ladder; I know many writers who began their careers by writing for non-paying markets and "forgot" to move past that. They became comfortable with the fact that non-paying markets are easier to please, and that it's much easier to get an acceptance this way. These writers didn't put enough value on their talents to announce to editors, "Thank you for the experience; I must now turn my efforts toward paying markets."

These writers are afraid to find out that their writing is "good enough" only if it's free. And there are, sadly, some writers who will never make a penny from their efforts because they are *not* cut out to be writers. These writers are purely hobbyists, even if they have deluded themselves into believing otherwise, and most of them populate the pages of pay-per-click web sites and vanity poetry anthologies.

If that's not you, it's time to distance yourself from that image. For just a minute, knock that inner critic down for the count and look at yourself honestly. Are you proud of what you write? Do you deserve a spot in a magazine? Would *you* read what you write? Would you enjoy it? Would you be eager to read your next piece?

If so, you owe it to yourself and to the rest of the world to get your work out there! Do your best to remember that this is a business; even though writing may be personal to you, whether or not your work gets accepted is purely a business issue. An editor has a limited amount of space to fill, and he or she has a specific agenda and specific tastes about the type of work she wants to fill those pages. Either your ideas and style fit, or they don't. If they don't, it doesn't mean they won't fit elsewhere. And if you're getting too many rejections, it may be that you're trying to fit a square peg into a round hole; that is, your work may fit in perfectly in a market you've overlooked, but it isn't appropriate for the type of market you keep approaching.

When I began freelancing, I was fresh out of college. I received rejection after rejection from general interest and health markets, and then it hit me like a pile of potatoes: I should be writing for college markets! And I made my first several sales, just like that. Because, even though I was too close to my own experiences to realize it, when I was 21, I wrote from the perspective of a 21-year-old. When I tried to "sound" 40, it was an act. When I just let myself be 21, the writing flowed much more naturally. I knew the needs of college students; I knew their lifestyle, their questions, their interests. As a recent graduate, I could even answer some of their questions with a bit of authority—questions like "How will I land a job after college? Are internships really important? How can I pay my way through graduate school?"

See if that applies to you. Are you overlooking obvious areas of expertise, or an understanding of a certain market demographic? Are you a parent? A cancer survivor? A gardener? A teacher? A hopeless romantic? An avid traveler? Just because you may not consider yourself an expert in any of these areas doesn't mean that you can't write for these markets, as we've discussed. If you have understanding and passion about a particular topic, chances are, you can write about it with much more insight than those who don't share your experiences.

It's time to be the confident, professional writer that you really are. It's time to submit your work—your best work—over and over until you achieve every one of your professional goals. Speaking of which, what *are* your goals?

Setting Goals

Instead of waiting for inspiration to hit, and running through your freelance career in a stream-of-consciousness fashion, be sure you've not only thought out, but written out, your career goals.

Break it down into short- and long-term goals, and update this list often. Short-term goals can be broken down by week or month, and long-term goals should be your plans for the next 6–12 months. Toward the beginning of my freelancing career, my list might have looked like this:

Short-Term Goals

Come up with three great ideas.

Do some research; conduct a preliminary interview.

Write and rewrite a great query letter for five to six markets.

Mail them out with SASEs and clips.

Move on and immediately start working on another idea.

Get at least four rejection letters.

Get a paying assignment.

Long-Term Goals

Get published in a major women's magazine.

Break into the health writing market.

Get a position as a regular romance columnist.

Once I had achieved all of those goals, I knew it was time to make some new ones! Now, my lists might look more like this:

Short-Term Goals

Negotiate for higher pay from regular clients.

Write a query for at least one magazine for which I've never written before.

Check in with editors to remind them I'm available for assignments.

Read several back issues of *Natural Health* at the library, and see if I can track down an editorial calendar.

Sell at least two reprints.

Long-Term Goals

Sell a cover story to *Natural Health*.

Become the first person editors think of when assigning health or relationships articles.

Apply for major grants to support investigative research for article series about organ transplant policies.

I bet the first thing you noticed was my seemingly-self deprecating, "Get at least four rejection letters" in the first set of short-term goals. But the truth is, it *was* a positive thing to get those rejection letters: It meant that I was brave enough and ambitious enough to send out at least four queries. And I knew that the more rejections I received, the more actively I was marketing my work, gaining insight into what didn't work, and getting closer to sales.

When you're still new to freelancing, it's good to narrow your focus. Notice in my original long-term goals, I said I wanted to write for a national women's magazine? I set that goal very purposefully; I didn't just say "any magazine." It had to be national, and it had to be a women's magazine. I knew the type of publication I was targeting, but I was careful not to get *too* specific, because then it would be too easy to fail. I didn't say I wanted to be published by *Redbook*. I was being honest with myself; I didn't know if I was qualified enough yet to write for them, and I didn't know if I had ideas appropriate for them, specifically. The goal was still a stretch, but it was more realistic for me to aim for a group of magazines rather than one in particular.

The story changed, though, in my second set of goals.

With experience and credits comes a new level of confidence and of mastery. Once I had many national magazine credits, I knew that my bio was no longer going to hold me back with nearly any publication. There were few editors who would question my professionalism, considering my experience. Therefore, not only could I aim higher, but I could aim more specifically. I had knocked down one of my fears ("Am I qualified enough?"), and therefore, I only had one fear left ("Do I have ideas appropriate for *Natural Health*, specifically?") Well, no. Not exactly. But that's why it's a long-term goal!

I know I will come up with an idea that's just perfect for them. And why? Because I've already read a few issues, and because in my short-term goals, I've committed to study them more closely to figure out exactly how to hit home with them.

Don't be afraid to think big with your goals—really big! You may even want to add different "levels" to your short- and long-term goals to accommodate your innermost desires without feeling like you're being unrealistic. For example, when I began writing, I would never have written, "Become one of the highest-paid freelance writers in the country" as one of my goals—short *or* long term—because it seemed so far away and presumptuous. But if I added in some new categories:

Short-Term Goals for the Week

Short-Term Goals for the Month

Long-Term Goals for the Year

Long-Term Goals for the Next 5 Years

Lifetime Goals

Well, then I could fit in my "best-paid freelancer" goal. It would be a lifetime goal, therefore feeling more acceptable to me. It would be a sign that I wasn't expecting to earn this one anytime soon, but I wanted to keep it on my radar screen for the far-off future.

Why is it important to write these goals down?

Because it will help you to stay focused and remember why you're working. It's very easy to get caught in a rut, where you're making enough money to get by, or you're writing about subjects that are in your "comfort zone." But what if you *really* wanted to write articles about a particular social cause, and you somehow became sidetracked into writing articles about horse care? Well, it may be time to look over your list of goals again and remember that you should move on.

Written goals will also help you feel you're on the right track whenever you can check one off. If your goal is to receive a personalized response from an editor rather than a form letter, you'll remember that this is an accomplishment when you check it off—even if it *is* a rejection letter! If you wrote down that you wanted to write your first feature article, when you're feeling insecure about your career later on, you can remember that you've already achieved things that were a challenge to you earlier.

It's important to give yourself little pats on the back for your accomplishments as a writer. When you work from home, there's no boss to congratulate you on your progress or tell you it's time for a promotion. There's only you. So be your own (nice) boss and tell yourself when it's time for a break, or when it's time to raise your rates, or when it's time to focus your energy on new projects. You can do that by taking some time to evaluate yourself every few months and set new goals that reflect your accomplishments.

ASSIGNMENT

My short-term goals for the week _____

_____

My short-term goals for the month _____

_____

My long-term goals for the year _____

_____

My long-term goals for the next five years _____

_____

My lifetime goals _____

_____

Your goals are uniquely yours, and always right!

Chapter 8
QUERIES IN THE WILD

Inside This Chapter

- **Dissecting a successful query**
- **Querying don'ts**
- **Other ways to pitch stories**

Queries That Work

Now that you know what queries are all about, it's time to look at some real-world situations and examples to examine what works, what doesn't work, and why.

This is an e-query of mine that sold to *Prevention*:

> **Dear Ms. Foley:**
>
> **Your 12-year-old daughter, Amy, hates her nose. You know she hates her nose, because she mentions it every 8.6 seconds. She's even saving up her allowance for plastic surgery, and she seems determined to stay miserable until she's old enough to get a nose job.**

Using second person helped me to address the reader, something I know *Prevention* likes; they say their most popular articles are the ones that are the most conversational. In this case, I didn't want to use a real-life Zimmerman. I felt it was important was to show that this "Amy" was not one specific redhead from Iowa, but rather, someone who might be your own daughter. Also, I'm showing that I know the target market: *Prevention's* readers are mostly 35 and older, so I didn't want to make Amy too young; most of this readership won't have very young children.

> **You, on the other hand, don't see anything wrong with her nose, or any other part of her. And because she isn't starving herself or binging and purging, you don't realize how unhealthy her appearance obsession may be.**

I've quickly made a comparison to the better-known appearance-related disorders—anorexia and bulimia—and made my point to the editor that what I'm about to discuss is just as unhealthy as they are.

> **Amy may suffer from body dysmorphic disorder (BDD), an anxiety disorder in which sufferers have a distorted negative image of their appearances; most people with the disorder become obsessed with changing a particular "bad" feature, and their self-esteem suffers because of it.**

There you have it: a succinct, simple definition. Here's what the disorder is.

> **According to psychologist J. Kevin Thompson, "In perhaps 70 percent of cases, the onset of symptoms begins in adolescence." A specific event often triggers the disorder; teasing from schoolmates or sexual abuse, for example.**

Here's when it happens and what sometimes causes it. And, hey, look, I've already done some research. As it turned out when I fully researched it later, that second sentence wasn't entirely accurate. Specific events sometimes trigger the event, but I'd no longer go so far as to say "often." But that's okay; queries aren't expected to be perfectly fact-checked like the articles themselves are. For this query, I learned enough to be reasonably well-versed on the topic, but I didn't spend weeks studying it until after I got the contract.

> **In its worst form, BDD can lead a person to isolate herself, become severely depressed, or even to commit suicide.**

See? I told you this was serious stuff, editor. Now I'm backing it up. You could save people's lives by running this article.

> **Xenia Madison suffered from BDD well into her twenties before she was properly diagnosed. "Ball games and other such situations with crowds were impossible because I was afraid I might be imperfect, and I couldn't let anyone see me that way." If her lipstick was bleeding or there was lint on her pants, she'd cancel appointments.**

> **Niki Taylor went so far as to have reconstructive surgery on her jawbone when she was in college, but it didn't help her body image. It wasn't until she saw a therapist that she was able to "make peace" with her appearance.**

Look, editor—you can have confidence in me. I've already done my homework and even found the "people on the street" to interview. Note: That's one of the toughest parts of articles like this, because it's not always easy to track people down who are willing to speak about potentially embarrassing experiences, and who can speak about it with insight and honesty. I already knew these two women because they contributed to my book *Conquering Panic and Anxiety Disorders*. In fact, I had never heard of BDD until I spoke to Xenia.

Note, too, that you can gain an edge with these "real people" stories because staff writers and top freelancers sometimes consider them to be a pain in the rear. Once you've found a specialty, you can build up a strong Rolodex full of experts you can call upon whenever you need a quotation about a particular topic—but you won't be able to flip through your files and instantly find three women who've conquered BDD and are willing to talk about it. For that, you'll have to do some digging. And at this point in your career, that's exactly what you should be doing to give yourself a leg up on your more experienced competition. Call psychologists and ask if they'll pass your name on to clients who might be willing to talk to a writer. Search on Internet message boards for people who are chatting about this topic. Find a newsletter list devoted to your subject and ask the moderator if you can send a request for interviewees out to the readers.

> **Luckily, Xenia, Niki, and many others have fully recovered. I would like to share the story of three such women, and offer tips from psychologists who specialize in body image disorders. I believe this article could open the eyes of many mothers, and help them recognize this disorder in their children (or in themselves!). Eating disorders are well-publicized, but BDD is not. May I share this article with your magazine's readers?**

Editor: This will be an uplifting article, and here's how it will help your readers. It's not well-publicized, which means I'm offering you a story that you and your competitors haven't already done to death.

> **I am a full-time writer with hundreds of articles published (in such publications as *Woman's World*, *Woman's Own*, *Writer's Digest*, and Salon.com), and eight books to be published by the end of 2003. My latest is *Conquering Panic and Anxiety Disorders* (Hunter House, November, 2002).**

I vary which credits I name based on the type of market I'm querying; if I'm approaching a men's magazine, I obviously mention the other men's magazines I've written for. I always mention that I'm a full-time writer so no one worries that I'm just a hobbyist who's not going to take deadlines seriously if something comes up in my "real" job.

> **I am an excellent researcher, work well with deadlines, and would love the chance to work with you. Thank you for your consideration.**

Leave Out the Kitchen Sink

I used to list pretty much every magazine that had ever published me, figuring that 30 magazines would look really impressive. That was a mistake. When you list more than five or six magazines, editors realize that those are probably all the magazines you've ever written for . . . not to mention that most of the 30 names I was giving were small-circulation or trade magazines and e-zines that wouldn't impress any big editors.

One of my students showed me a query she was sending, and her bio said something like this: "I have written for The Flagstaff Times, The Flagstaff Library News, Flagstaff Business Journal, *and I received the Flagstaff Award of Excellent Journalism in 1988." A little tweaking, and her new bio read, "I am an award-winning writer with credits from several daily and weekly newspapers. I regularly contribute to* The Flagstaff Times." *What's the difference? Well, when all of your credits are local, it makes you sound like a small-potatoes writer. Never lie, but you don't need to specifically point out that you've never written for a national publication, and you don't need to include dates when they're not in your favor.*

I don't always add this kind of note; it depends on the vibe I've gotten from the editor. In this case, I had just sent her my first query and she responded within a day to tell me she liked the idea but it was too late in the year to assign a winter-themed piece. So I knew I already had a shot with her. Now I wanted to find every way I could to give her the confidence to hire me for the first time.

Consider Your Sources

Karen Roman, editor of a computer technology/small business magazine, suggests that it helps to list your resources when querying for nonfiction articles. She explains that she is much more likely to hire someone if she knows she can count on accurate information and quotations. You may wish to note which experts you plan to quote and why they're qualified—for example, in my last query, I could have gotten specific and written, "I plan to interview Katharine A. Phillips, MD, director of the Body Dysmorphic Disorder and Body Image Program at Butler Hospital; Randall Flanery, PhD, a child psychologist and professor of community and family medicine at St. Louis University's School of Medicine; and Dean M. Toriumi, MD, president of the American Academy of Facial Plastic and Reconstructive Surgery."

Further, Karen notes that if queries sound at all self-serving (coming off like a press release for a company or individual), she would never assign the piece.

"My advice is to be honest about what you can provide, when it will be available, and be sure it fits the format of magazine," she says. "In short, what I find irresistible is a sense that I can trust the writer to make good on his or her clear promise to deliver relevant content in a professional manner. Vague (or misspelled!) queries always send up a red flag."

Things NOT to Do in Query Letters

Beware of Overselling

"Say what you mean, mean what you say, then shut up," says Deborah J. Miller, freelance writer for 18 years.

Less is more. Give them the ol' one-two punch and get out of there, fast. Your letter should have plenty of white space. The fewer words you give editors, the less ground you give them to reject you. Watch this train wreck:

> **Dear Mr. Editor:**
>
> **"The happier you keep your employees, the happier they will keep the customers," says Joe Schmoe, owner of the Squeaky Clean Car Wash in Somewhereville, New York. Since Joe bought the car wash more than 12 years ago, he has had a remarkably low employee turnover rate, and he attributes this to his "human" approach to management. He has enacted a system of incentives, rotations, and perks that keep his workers loyal.**

Editor thinks: "Fine so far. The writer has introduced the subject, and it's pretty clear what the article will be about: a smart businessman's tips for increasing employee satisfaction and loyalty. Since I edit a publication meant for small business owners, it seems like a pretty good idea for my readers."

> **For example, he offers attendants a commission for selling "extras," such as hot wax, polish wax, rust inhibitors, and undercarriage pressure washing. Since he began this system, employees are more motivated to make consumers aware of all of the services this car wash offers. In turn, the ratio of customers who purchase extra services versus those who opt for regular washes has more than doubled. Translation: Everyone wins.**

Editor thinks: "Not bad. The writer's given me a tease about what specific tips will be discussed, and what original ideas this businessman can offer the readership. I'm curious to learn more about what Joe has done. There's concrete evidence that this man's techniques work (because the customers are buying twice as many extra services)."

> **Joe is a really nice guy, and he's very eager to be interviewed for your magazine.**

Editor thinks: "Uh . . . what? Who cares? And why is he so eager? Now I'm wondering about Joe's motives—is this going to come across like an advertisement?"

> **Joe's techniques have been discussed in *Business Monthly Magazine*, *This Week In Business*, *Entrepreneurs 'R Us*, and BusinessOwner.com.**

Editor thinks: "Wait a minute. You mean this is old news? If his techniques have already been covered by some of my competitors, I don't want to re-hash old material."

> **I can also interview Joe's customers to talk about how much they like his service.**

Editor thinks: "What does this have to do with anything? That's totally irrelevant to this piece. Maybe I was wrong about this writer—it doesn't sound like she is a very clear thinker."

> **Buy this article from me, fast, before your competition does. Joe's techniques will revolutionize the way business is done!**

Editor thinks: "What is this, a threat? I've seen this technique before—the 'this is a blockbuster article and you'd better hire me fast, because everyone in town wants this piece' technique. It always makes me think the exact opposite—that the writer is full of hooey, that the article must be so lame that it can't stand on its own (without the writer telling me how great it is), and that the writer will be difficult to work with. This writer is obviously an amateur."

> **I was the editor of my college newspaper and a regular contributor to our Students In The News section. I even won an award from the Collegiate Press.**

Editor thinks: "Yep, I was right. I need coffee. I want to maim this writer for wasting my time. I hope she gets a computer virus."

> **Thank you so much for taking the time to read my letter. I would really like to write for your magazine, and I hope you'll give me the chance. I'll work hard to prove that I deserve this piece . . .**

Editor throws query and SASE in trash. But first, he steals your stamp and re-pastes it on someone else's acceptance letter.

Post-Mortem

This writer almost had the job. The editor was interested right away, and the writer sustained that interest through the second paragraph. It's only when the writer started grasping at straws, trying too hard to prove the credibility and importance of this piece, that she fell on her face.

Can't you smell the desperation growing in this letter?

Never hard-sell anything, and never tell an editor that your idea is great. Let him come to that conclusion himself, through the strength of your writing.

And don't let punctuation talk for you. Let the strength of your message come from your words, not your screaming punctuation, fancy formatting, or bright orange envelope.

The Meek Don't Inherit the Magazines

While you must beware of being overly grand and shouting your ideas into the editor's ears, writing query letters that apologize for their very existence are just as much of a disservice to you. There is no need to begin the letter with a mousy greeting like, "I am an aspiring writer, and I'd appreciate it if you'd take the time to read my letter and see if you think I might be a good candidate for your magazine." Similarly, there is no need to end the letter with gushy, "you're my last hope" pleas to the editor.

Beware of mouse language: "I think," "I might," "I hope," "aspiring," "can I," and "may I" are all mouse terms. You're offering a product: your article. Your only function here is to present your product in a desirable light and see if the buyer needs your product right now. The letter should leave the impression that you are hopeful, but not desperate to sell this piece to this market.

I am often amazed at the lack of self-confidence demonstrated in queries that are sent my way. Here's an example of a query I once received (identifying information changed):

> **I'm a newspaper reporter (*Idaho Daily*) and an aspiring fiction writer. Of course, I have a big stack o' rejection slips from various fiction mags. And that's not even counting the magazines that never even bothered to send me a rejection letter.**
>
> **However, I do have several years journalism experience. I've also freelanced video reviews to the *Video Review Magazine*. I have a journalism degree from BlahBlah University.**
>
> **Basically, I'd love to write movie reviews for your web site. Let me know.**
>
> **Thanks for your time.**
>
> **Sincerely,**
>
> **Writer**

What did this letter tell me? That this guy had been rejected all over the place. Why in the world would he announce that to me? Did he want me to hire him out of pity? Forget it. I want the Best of the Best on my staff. I don't want to use writers who can't find work. Sure, he may be a terrific writer who's either (a) very unlucky, or (b) just bad at writing queries, but I don't have the time to waste finding out.

He just sent me a three-paragraph letter, and of that whole letter, only one sentence told me what he wanted to write. ("Basically, I'd love to write movie reviews for your web site.") Why did I wade through his credits (or lack thereof) and education before he even mentioned what he wanted to do for me? I don't care about credits until *after* I've seen the pitch. If the pitch stinks, I don't need to bother reading any further. It doesn't matter to me if the writer holds a Pulitzer Prize if his idea doesn't fit my publication.

Here's another query falling in the "don't do this" category:

> **Dear Jenna,**
>
> **I'm a freelance music critic for the Such and Such Newspaper, and I've written a number of essays on the critic's life.**
>
> **Before you start snoring, I want to assure you that they are funny and informative. At least that's what my mom tells me.**
>
> **Would you be interested in looking at one?**
>
> **Thanks,**
>
> **Writer**

First, the pet peeve: this writer doesn't know me. Why did he use my first name? I realize that my site is (intentionally) friendly, and I probably come across as a nice, informal gal. But when you're asking an editor to look at your work, show respect. You can use first names *after* you get the assignment. It won't make or break my decision on this query, of course, but it is an annoyance.

Here's the query's larger problem, however: I wasn't snoring. Why would I be? His topic is perfect for my web site. Of course I'd be interested in hearing

---

Sell it Fast and Furiously

Get to the nitty-gritty first. Intrigue the editor from the first sentence, and she'll keep reading. Save the details of what you're proposing and where it might fit for the end of the letter. "Sell it to me in the first three lines," says Chandra Czape of Ladies' Home Journal.

about the life of a critic. However, when he says, "Before you start snoring," I think three things:

1. Wait. *Should* I be snoring? Is this a boring topic? Will my readers be bored by it?
2. If *he* thought his hook was boring, why did he send it to me? Why didn't he rewrite it until he was sure it was going to sound fascinating?
3. How in the world does he plan to convey enough enthusiasm in the essay to warrant a reader's enthusiasm if he thinks the topic sounds boring?

I've read many queries and submissions with some variation of "before you start snoring." One of my columnists began his first submission with, "What a change. To think someone will actually be reading my writing!" I asked him to ax that, because it immediately makes the reader think, "Well, if no one else wants to read what this guy has to say, why should I? What's wrong with the writer, and why he can't get read elsewhere?"

What a great disservice to do to your work!

If you're about to send out a query or a submission, you'd better be very confident that it's a great representation of your best work. If that's the case, *do not* package it in a tone of self-loathing!

Writers are a neurotic breed who can go from feeling like the Greatest Writer Who Ever Lived to worrying they're illiterate tree stumps in the course of three minutes, but for the purpose of the query, leave your ego out of it altogether. It's not about you. It's about your story.

By all means, convey your passion about a topic. But don't bother telling your prospective editor that your idea is great, unique, Earth-shattering, boring, or anywhere in between. Let the editor decide that on her own. Your job is to make her believe your idea is fascinating and relevant without ever telling her it's fantastic and relevant. Do this by letting whatever it is about the topic that interests *you* come through clearly in your letter.

Other Pitching Situations
Answering a general "writers wanted" ad

Sometimes, a publication will put out a general call for writers without asking for queries. In situations like this, it usually means that they already have plenty of ideas generated in-house and are looking to make assignments.

In cases like that, it's fine to include one or more article ideas of your own (in fact, it's smart to do so, because it can show that you understand their publication's focus). More important in this situation, however, are your personal statements and credentials. Spend more time explaining your specialties and availability. A response to a call for writers from a new college magazine might look like this:

Dear Ms. Harper:

I read your call for writers at AbsoluteWrite.com, and I'm very interested in writing for your publication.

I am a freelance writer with experience writing for a college market. I have written for *U Magazine*, *College Leaders*, and *Campus Life*. In addition, I wrote a regular column for *New England Parents* about preparing for children's college education.

My oldest son graduated from New York University last spring, and my daughter is currently enrolled at Cornell. Their experiences provide me with a wealth of new story ideas, and they keep me in touch with the current college environment.

I am available for assignments, and I can work with fast deadlines. If you are also interested in seeing original story ideas, I have enclosed a list of three article topics that I'd love to write for you. I have also included two clips of my work.

You can reach me by phone at (xxx) xxx-xxxx anytime after 10 a.m. I wish you the best with your new publication, and I hope to work with you soon.

Best wishes,

Writer

The multiple topic query

This is not a technique I use often, but I know a few freelancers who regularly send more than one idea at a time to a publication.

I find that it's best to keep focused on one idea at a time for one simple reason: If you present three or four unrelated ideas at once, an editor may choose one and forget the others. This is especially true if you're new to the publication: The editor needs to "audition" you with the first piece, so it's unlikely that you'll get more than one assignment at once with a new market. However, if you send one idea now, and more ideas after you've already successfully completed the first assignment, you may land assignments for all of your ideas.

The only time I query with multiple ideas is when I've written for the publication already. By then, the formalities have slipped away, and I can send a note with much-less-detailed queries, and possibly win multiple assignments. Here's an example:

Hi Jack,

I'm so glad you liked the piece, and, yes, I would love to write for you again. Are you only interested in "small town" people for profiles? I thought of another good candidate, but he's in Albany. He opened "Steamer No. 10," a children's theatre, in an old firehouse, and uses it to put on shows to educate kids about local and world history (shows about Nellie Bly, the Erie Canal, etc.). The troupe also tours elementary schools, putting on performances to enhance classroom learning. He's a real one-man force, often paying actors from his own pocket as he writes the scripts, builds sets, does sound and lighting, pops the popcorn, answers the phones, directs, etc. I'd love to profile him if you see fit.

Also, I have a perfect "Hometown Hero" for the Christmas week edition. I'm sure you already have something slated, but I'm wondering if you might want to rearrange. Here's why:

Mike Brandt is as close to Santa Claus as you'll likely ever see. He's a white-haired, white-bearded, plump man with small rectangular spectacles from Sayville, NY. Everywhere he goes, every day, people whisper and children squeal with excitement. Mike has been playing "Santa" every Christmas for more than 25 years. He does guest appearances for fire departments, charity events, food shelters, etc., as well as private parties. He loves the fact that he looks like the perfect image of Santa Claus and says that the main joy in his life is the Christmas season.

If you're interested, I can get the article to you by Monday night. I even have photos—or I can give you his contact info if you want to use your own photographer.

Let me know what you think.

Regards,

Jenna

Freelancer Mike Sedge likes to send out occasional "brochures" with a list of a dozen or more story topics to several publications at once. Although he says he doesn't get a lot of assignments for the specific ideas he proposes, he says the brochure always gets attention, and he often winds up getting phone calls from editors who will then assign him something of their choosing. I wouldn't pull this with major magazines; it shows that you're not targeting ideas specifically for their publications, and it shows that you're shopping the same ideas all over the place. But if you're targeting regional magazines or newspapers and you feel like being gutsy, this might be fun to try.

Other writers I know write "thank you" notes or cards after completing an assignment, then slip in a note with additional story ideas.

Querying for a regular column

Does writing a regular column sound like your bag? You'll need to write a query that gives a hook, then an overview of your entire column rather than just one piece. As opposed to writing a query letter for a one-time assignment, you will have to include at least two or three sample columns on spec for this one, unless this is an editor you've worked with many times. In that case, you might be able to skip the samples and just include the description and a few summaries.

It's unlikely for you to land a column with a publication you've never written for before, so try to publish at least one article with the magazine before you go for the column pitch.

This is a nice feather to add to your cap, though, if you can land it. Editors like to see pitches from writers who are columnists somewhere-or-other, because it shows that the publication trusts your writing skill, wants to work with you regularly, and you know how to meet deadlines.

You'll find many situations in which you'll need to use a variation of your pitch. No matter how you approach it, however, the query remains the key to becoming a well-paid freelance writer. Master this craft, and you'll soon find you have more assignments than you can handle.

Targeting Versus Thunderstorming

Of all the things I wish I had learned earlier about freelancing, this is the big one: Targeting your queries is the most important thing you can do to boost your career.

You may have written the tightest, most wonderful, most intriguing query letter, but if the topic and angle aren't custom-tailored to the market you're querying, you might as well have finger-painted "hire me" on a piece of toilet paper and sent it on to the editor.

Let me assure you that sending out bulk mailings of the same query is truly ineffective. You may generate a sale by chance, but you will increase your odds considerably by offering a piece that is designed individually for a particular market. You will also endear yourself to editors if you don't waste their time with form letters that don't fit the specifications of their magazine.

Imagine buying a prom dress. You see a beautiful one, but it comes in only sizes 4 and 6, and you're a size 8. Now it doesn't matter how beautiful the dress is; it's just not going to fit you. Don't frustrate the heck out of editors by sending them beautiful prom dresses in the wrong sizes.

Getting Columnized

Here's what you need to include in a column proposal:

➤ *Description of your overall column*

➤ *Approximate word count*

➤ *Can you provide visuals?*

➤ *What frequency do you propose (weekly, monthly, etc.)?*

➤ *Do you have an established readership or name recognition in your field?*

➤ *Why is this column relevant to their readership, or how does it fill an editorial gap?*

➤ *If you're not including samples, then you must include several summaries of column topics.*

Here's an example:

Dear Ms. Smith:

Since when does romance have anything to do with finance?

Too many people are under the mistaken notion that they have to spend lots of money to do something romantic for their spouses or "significant others." On the contrary, most of the expensive, traditional symbols for romance (roses, jewelry, fancy dinners) are too overdone and generic to truly show your lover what's in your heart.

Instead, why not put down the wallet, and use your own two hands to create something unique, creative, and truly romantic?

In my column, "Hand-Made Romance: Crafty Tips For Loving Gifts," I'll offer one project for men, and one project for women each month. Each of these projects is inexpensive, uncomplicated, and guaranteed to bring smiles to the faces of the lucky recipients. I can also provide a photo of each of the completed crafts.

They run approximately 400 words, and can be delivered via email with high-resolution digital photos or as hard copies. I am the co-author of the book Crafty Loving, *which has sold more than 100,000 copies, and I've been interviewed on many television networks, including Lifetime, ABC, and FOX, so your readers may well recognize me. I noticed in your writers' guidelines that you're looking to add more relationships material, so I hope this will fit the bill.*

Enclosed are three sample columns. I look forward to your response.

Regards,

Writer

As a new freelancer, you have no reputation. Your job is to make sure that every mark on your freelancing record is a positive one. That starts with your first query letter.

According to WriterOnline.us editor T.M. Wright, "Even if the piece being submitted isn't right for Writer Online, if the query letter shows some flair, some dash, some verve, some sex (not literally, of course—we ARE a PG-rated e-zine), chances are my interest will be piqued."

Wright explains that even if the proposed article isn't appropriate for them, the writer can land a different assignment based on a great query. "The writer isn't simply trying to sell her article with her query letter, she's also selling her ability as a writer. Good writers are hard to find!"

While there is no shortage of people who call themselves writers, know that nearly all magazine editors are still on the hunt—which means that T.M. must be telling the truth. Good writers are a rare breed. Make a great impression with that query, and you might just find yourself a market for life.

ASSIGNMENT

 You're planning to query an editor of a women's magazine. You want to write an article that was inspired by an event you just witnessed. You saw a child shoplifting, and you noticed her mother wasn't watching. You alerted the mother as they exited the store. The mother scolded the child, but she didn't bring back the merchandise.

Which of these sentences could belong in your query, and which ones should you omit? Cross out the sentences that don't belong here.

1. "The child fingered the lip gloss, then slid it into her back pocket as her mother spoke to a saleslady nearby."

2. "In a 2003 study, the American Youth Association discovered that 40 percent of children under the age of 17 have shoplifted at least once."

3. "This kind of thing happens every day, but I thought it was interesting to see it first-hand."

4. "As I watched the mother leave the store, I realized no lesson had been imparted. She didn't make the child bring back the lipstick."

5. "If your magazine runs stories about parenting, I think this would be an excellent fit."

6. "I've worked as a day care attendant, and I've witnessed many ways that children sneak away with things that don't belong to them."

7. "The article will offer tips for parents who want to teach their children why shoplifting is wrong."

8. "Although I haven't been published before, I have two kids, and I know a lot about how difficult it can be to watch every move they make."

9. "A lot of kids shoplift, so this information will be useful to parents everywhere."

10. "I plan to interview reputed child psychologist Jan Smith, author of *How To Get Your Kids To Listen*; and Joe Brown from '*Town Business*,' an authority on how shoplifting affects businesses and paying customers."

If you crossed out numbers 3, 5, 8 and 9, you made me proud.

Here's why:

3. "This kind of thing happens every day . . . "

Could you be more imprecise? What happens every day? Shoplifting? Children shoplifting? Mothers not returning things their children shoplifted? And, sure, all three of those things happen every day. Get some real stats. Just how often do children shoplift? How much money do stores lose each year due to shoplifting? Which items do children tend to shoplift? And the "I thought it was interesting" thing—big deal. Magazines don't print stories they think are "interesting." They print stories that are fascinating, but they don't want to hear that you think it's fascinating: They want to be fascinated all by themselves based on what you tell them, not based on your opinion.

5. "If your magazine runs stories about . . . "

Why doesn't the writer know if the magazine runs those kinds of stories? If the writer hasn't taken the time to learn what kind of articles are appropriate, why should the editor take the time to consider this proposal? Don't let on that you aren't a regular reader, unless it would be nearly impossible for you to get your hands on a copy of the magazine. For example, I once queried a regional fishing magazine in Pennsylvania. I don't live in Pennsylvania, so I surmised the editor wouldn't get huffy if I asked a question that showed I hadn't read the magazine. In my first letter to him, I asked if his publication ran destination pieces, because I'd love to send him a pitch about a fishing resort. Not only did he not mind the question, but he referred me to another editor within his publishing company, too.

8. "Although I haven't been published before . . . "

Never mention that you haven't been published. Leave out the first part of the sentence, and just tell why you are qualified to write this article. The fact that you're a parent certainly helps. What else might qualify you? Have you researched this topic? Have you worked in retail and seen people try to shoplift before? In this case, it's based on something you've actually seen, so you don't need to work very hard to convince anyone that you know enough about the actual event to write about it, but you will have to convince them that you can provide expert tips for parents. You'll need an "expert" (like a child psychologist) to back you up.

9. "A lot of kids shoplift . . . "

Too vague. Take some initiative and do a little research first. Find accurate figures: It shows that you know how to find information, and a fact is always more powerful than an assumption. Further, don't quote a figure from an unreliable source. Get it from a recognizable and verifiable source. Fact-checkers exist to make sure that you aren't providing falsified, unreliable, or misquoted information. Don't blow it by vouching for the wrong "authority."

Chapter 9
REPRINTS AND SPIN-OFFS

Inside This Chapter

- **Querying for reprints**
- **Knowing your rights**
- **Querying for spin-offs**
- **Building on your experience**

Recycling Your Work

After you've published an article, assuming you've kept the rights, you get to sell it again. And again. This is called a reprint. If you take the same basic research and turn it into a new article, that's called a spin-off, rewrite, or reslant.

Reprints and spin-offs are often the lifeblood of freelance writers. It's enormously difficult to make a living (and keep sane) trying to find brand new ideas every day, research them, package them, and market them.

The rules are different when you're querying for a reprint versus an original article. You may notice that many markets claim not to accept reprints (as noted in guidelines or *Writer's Market* listings). This isn't always true. You can often make a case for your reprint, especially if it has only run in non-competing publications. For example, if your article ran only in your hometown newspaper, or in a specialized magazine, a general interest web site or non-overlapping regional magazine/newspaper shouldn't have a problem reprinting it.

Reprint fees are "found money." In what other field can you get paid extra for work you've already done for someone else? Beginning writers often overlook this area when they come up with article ideas, but you should *always* consider how many ways you can reprint, repackage, reslant, rewrite, and resell your articles. "I feel unhappy if an article hasn't been resold three times," says Roberta Beach Jacobson, a freelancer who's written for publications such as *Woman's Day*, *McCall's*, and *Natural Home*.

Reprints don't pay as well as original articles, of course. Expect to receive about half of the fee usually paid for original articles at that publication. But reprint rights are non-exclusive, so you can resell the article to several publications all at once.

If you're tremendously lucky, sometimes a publication will seek you out and ask to reprint an article. *Reader's Digest* and *Utne Reader* are both well-known for this; they're very prestigious publications, and they are largely reprint markets. However, most of the time, the mountain doesn't come to Mohammed, and you'll have to send them a query to alert them to your article's presence.

Querying for a reprint is really a bit of a misnomer—you're not querying in the same sense that you would for an original article. You're going to include the actual submission, so it's more of a cover letter.

This letter doesn't have to be anywhere near as in-depth as an original query, because you're including the piece. All that's required is a very short hook and description, followed by the rights available and note about where the piece has run. If you're offering anything in addition to the article (photos, graphics, sidebar), make note of this, too. In almost all cases, publications buy only one-time rights to your photographs, so you can reuse them without worry unless your contract states otherwise. You can also offer new photos or new sidebars with your reprint.

If you write anything original for the reprint market, be sure to get a separate fee for it! In other words, if they ask you to add in a new sidebar, or to expand the article, negotiate for extra money beyond the reprint fee. If the publications asks for very minor changes or edits that don't require you to do much additional research or writing, this still counts as a reprint. For example, if the editor wants you to add in a paragraph explaining something you just touched on, or wants you to add a regional slant to the piece, consider it part of the reprint fee. If they ask for major changes, it's probably a rewrite (spin-off), and you should expect to be paid for it as an original article. More on this in the "spin-offs" section.

The biggest "trick" in selling a reprint is making a case for offering them used goods. You'll have to explain why this is just as good as a fresh, new article by suggesting that the vast majority of their readers won't have seen it elsewhere. Here are a few examples of statements I've used:

➤ (To a print magazine): This article has only run online at a small web site for pediatricians: Fluff-n-udder.com. First print rights are available.

➤ (To a regional magazine): This article circulated only in the Denver area, originally appearing in *Fluff-n-udder* magazine. First rights are available in New York.

➤ (To a consumer magazine): Although the article has been published within the trade sector, it has never appeared in a consumer magazine.

➤ (To a magazine in England): This article has been published only in the United States.

➤ (To a magazine with a corresponding web site): This article first appeared in *Fluff-n-udder* newspaper (circulation: 5,000). Second print and first electronic rights are available.

Any rights you haven't contractually sold, you still own. So if an e-zine asked you for electronic rights, you can still sell first print rights in any country, and if a newspaper bought first North American serial rights only, you can still sell reprint (or "second print," which means the same thing) rights in North America, first rights in other countries, and electronic rights.

You may even wish to add in a more direct statement following your rights statement, to the effect of: "It is very unlikely that your readers will have seen this piece elsewhere."

If you can't make a claim like the one above, all is not lost. Some publications are not concerned if your article has run in overlapping markets. It's certainly worth the effort to try—you've already written the piece, so your only risk is the time you'll spend writing cover letters and photocopying, and the cost of postage.

You may have noticed a funny statement earlier: "First rights are available in New York." Can you make up your own rights? Absolutely! If you can pull it off, it can be very advantageous to you, and reassuring to your client.

How so? You can offer them exclusivity for their demographic, while retaining the right to resell the piece to other markets. Whenever you make the first sale, do your very best to negotiate to keep as many rights as possible. The simple rule is this: Give the publication whatever rights it *needs* at an appropriate cost. If they demand all rights, they'd better be prepared to pay for them. Be aware that you won't be allowed to resell that article again in any form, even if you write a book one day and want to incorporate the article into a chapter, or even if the magazine folds (you may be able to get reprint rights back in this case, but you'd have to get that in writing from the publisher, because the magazine could re-launch or be sold to another publisher sometime in the future).

Magazines, newspapers, and newsletters are known as *serials*, meaning that they're periodicals published on a set schedule. Therefore, when you see the word "serial" crop up in your contracts, you know that the magazine is purchasing the right to print your article in a periodical as opposed to a book or on a web site. First North American serial rights (FNASR) are the most commonly requested by magazine publishers, but even that isn't always necessary. Try to negotiate to narrow the rights down to region or target market whenever possible (e.g., first serial rights within the technology sector, or first serial rights in the teen audience marketplace).

If an editor is concerned about the possibility that you'll sell to her competition, ask for a list of competitors, and add a statement to your contract that you promise not to offer your article to any of them. Or stipulate a period of time, such as, "exclusive rights for three (or six) months, non-exclusive rights thereafter."

If you've done this, then you've made your job much easier when it comes to selling reprints. Recently, I sold the same essay to four regional parenting magazines. Three of them simply asked for one-time rights, which leaves me free to sell reprints wherever I like. One asked for one-time rights and exclusivity within the Dallas/Fort Worth area for the month of December. Quite reasonable; my only limitation now is that I may not allow any other print publication in that area to run the piece during that month.

If you're querying by mail, include a sharp photocopy of the article as it appeared in the original publication. Be absolutely certain that the type is legible; if not, then also include a typed version from your computer, as you would send an original manuscript. If querying by email, copy and paste the article into the body of the message, including the name of the publication and date it first appeared in parentheses at the bottom (*Maxim*, October, 2004).

But They'll Never Know

A common question:

"If I've sold rights only in New York/to the teen market/online, then can I sell first North American serial rights elsewhere, pitching it as if it's an original article?"

Unfortunately, no. Once the article has been published, it's been published, and you run the risk of being sued if your editor happens to stumble across

What Counts as Published?

If it was published in your library or church bulletin, your company newsletter, an anthology, an underground 'zine, or a "letter to the editor" in your local paper, yes, it's been published. Even though most of these don't count as professional credits, you still cannot sell first rights to any of these pieces again; you must inform the editor where and when the piece first ran. Note that it is highly unlikely an editor will turn a piece down if you say, "This article was published only in my church newsletter, which reaches 300 people in Allston, Massachusetts." It is even less likely that the editor will mind if you tell her that the first two paragraphs are from that church newsletter, but the rest of it is rewritten.

the piece elsewhere. This applies even if it was only printed in your high school paper 20 years ago. The chances of anyone ever catching you are extremely remote, but that is the rule and your reputation is on the line. You can offer first rights within each specific demographic, but not FNASR. You can, however, sell something abroad, and then offer FNASR in the United States. (Or sell it here first, and then offer first British serial rights, first Australian serial rights, and so on.)

So, be forthcoming about where the piece has run. If it has run in more than one publication, you need only list the place it originally appeared, but you can't fib about the scope of its appearances. There are clever ways of downplaying it, however.

For example, even if your article has appeared on 20 different web sites, but never in print, you can make this honest statement: "It has been published electronically only, originally appearing at Fluff-n-udder.com."

Ditto for the reverse situation; it may have been syndicated to 100 different newspapers, but if it's never run online, you can still offer first electronic rights and mention only the original newspaper in which it ran.

The only exception to this rule is if you've "published" the piece on your own web site or in your own media kit/brochure as a sample of your work, and even that isn't 100 percent safe. If your web site is popular and you don't make the clear distinction that this is an unpublished writing sample, you may have trouble. But if it's just a small site, it's only to promote your own writing (a "virtual résumé"), and you've marked the sample as such, you should be able to rest easy and sell FNASR later. To be safe, you should take the article off your web site as soon as a publication offers to buy it, and not put it back until after the publication has run it.

Liar, Liar, Pants on Fire

"I have a friend who is an editor at a major women's mag, which shares office space with another mag owned by the same company," says Bobbi Dempsey, *freelancer for magazines like* Good Housekeeping *and* Parents. *"This editor once received a pitch that caught her interest, so she asked the writer if she'd pitched it to any other mags. The writer said 'no.' Lo and behold, shortly after that, this editor glanced at the computer of her office-mate (an editor at another mag) and spotted the very same query from the writer who had claimed she hadn't submitted it elsewhere. Needless to say, that writer didn't get the assignment (or any others) from this editor."*

As an editor, I ran into a problem once with this situation. A writer wrote a great article for Writer Online, and I was planning to use it in an upcoming issue. This writer also ran a small web site for screenwriters. I went to her web site one day, and found the article posted there, with the note "Reprinted with permission from WriterOnline.net." That made me angry: We hadn't run the piece yet, so it certainly wasn't "reprinted," and definitely not with my permission! Considering our markets were overlapping, I didn't want my readers to have seen this piece elsewhere before they saw it at ours. After all, I was paying for that right. I asked the writer to remove the article until after we ran it, and she did. But it left a bad impression; I would probably think twice before hiring that writer again, because I'd worry that she wasn't being forthcoming about whether or not the piece was original.

One caveat to selling a reprint to a market that doesn't usually accept reprints: You may be asked to name your own fee.

Editors who aren't used to running reprints may not have a set guideline for fees. I ran into this situation a few times, and once dropped the ball terribly. I offered a health-related reprint to a little-known web site. They accepted and asked for my fee. I searched around for guidelines, but couldn't find them. I asked for $125, figuring she'd try to talk me down to $100. As soon as she happily agreed, I knew I must have undercharged. Sure enough, when I got my first assignment for an original article from the same editor, I was offered their standard flat rate: $600. This means I should have asked for $300 for the reprint. Live and learn: Now I do more background checks when I'm asked to name a fee. I check in at all the writers' sites and ask around to find out if others have

---

In the end, your reprint letter should look something like this:

Dear Ms. Jones:

I'd like to offer the following article about the dangers of tooth decay for your consideration. The article addresses less commonly understood secondary health problems that may arise from bad dental health (such as sinus infections, headaches, etc.). It originally ran at Fluff-n-udder.com (a web site for new parents) in November 2003, and is available for reprint.

I am a freelance writer with credits from a variety of publications, recently including Suchandsuch, ThisOtherMag, and BoDiddley. I also served as the food editor for SomeNewspaper from 1999 to 2003. I look forward to your response.

Regards,

Writer

written for that publication before, and what they were paid. Last week, I wrote a note to a member of one of my writing groups and told him I had a tacky question: A newspaper he had written for wanted to know my fee for an op-ed, and I wanted to know if he'd tell me what he got paid for columns there. He was happy to share, so I was able to name a price that was in an appropriate range for the newspaper (about $70).

Now, onto the most cost-effective use of your writing time: spin-offs and rewrites.

Writers often wonder what constitutes a spin-off versus a reprint. The best answer I can give is more common sense than strict rule: The article must be significantly different to qualify as a spin-off. If you've written an article about the current state of the NASA space program for an adult publication, can you then use some of your research to write a biography of a specific astronaut for a teen magazine? Absolutely. Can you reuse some of the same quotations? Yes—but don't get carried away. If you've done your research, you should have plenty of material that didn't make it into the first article but can be used in this one.

Adding in a few sentences or changing a couple of examples does not constitute a rewrite.

I came across a writer's résumé on the Internet. Her credits were few and not all that impressive, but this woman was a master at spin-offs. What were her clips? Nearly all of them were "Top Ten Movies About _____." That is, she

Ways to Recycle an Article
- *Write the piece for a different audience (different age group, sex, trade, personality type, etc.).*
- *Condense it or expand it.*
- *Pick one person, fact, or event of interest within the article to use as the focus for the next piece.*
- *Find a local angle—or, conversely, if it was a local piece, find a national or international angle.*
- *If it was a nonfiction article, write a personal essay/editorial about your impressions.*
- *Argue the other point. (Example: If it was an article about the need for more discipline in children's lives, write about why children need more independence.)*
- *If the original was largely factual in nature, make it anecdotal, and vice-versa.*
- *Take your transcripts and offer the piece as an interview.*

might have written a "Top Ten Movies Featuring Architects" for an architecture magazine, a "Top Ten Movies About Weddings" for a bridal magazine, a "Top Ten Movies About Getting High" for a counterculture magazine, and so on. Presumably these are fun articles that don't require much research, and this woman has just created a cottage industry for herself. Feasibly, she could come up with 10 movies on just about any subject. Or get even more specific—the top 10 most delectable-looking cakes ever featured in a movie for a baker's magazine, or the top 10 pick-up lines in movies for a men's magazine.

Immediately, I began thinking about what I could do like this, and I came up with "Weird Items on eBay." Don't steal this from me, because I'm actually planning to use it—I can come up with a listing of the Top 10 Weirdest/Coolest/Kinkiest Items on eBay for a variety of markets. I might write a "Top 10 Weirdest Music-Related Items on eBay" for a music magazine, highlighting things like the auction for a lock of Little Richard's hair or a badly scratched Magic Garden album that's being sold as a coaster. I could write a "Top 10 Most Perverse Items on eBay" for an adult magazine, talking about the college girl who's selling her stinky old sneakers to foot fetishists and the person selling his used blow-up doll. Sure, I could simply write these "articles" as lists and no more, but if I wanted to increase the word count, I might track down the people buying and selling these things and ask them why they're doing so, what they plan to do with the items, where they got the items, and so on. And I might interview a shrink to tell me why someone might buy these things in the first place.

(Update: I sent that query to *Playboy*, and they're interested. Keep your fingers crossed for me.)

Spin-Off Queries

Querying for spin-offs is essentially the same as querying for an original, with one million-dollar question attached: do you mention the original article?

First of all, you have no obligation to do so, so if it makes you uncomfortable to mention that you've written something similar, leave it out. However, it can usually work to your benefit because it establishes your credentials and expertise to write this piece.

By adding in a line that says, "I have written about this topic before for XYZ Magazine," you can improve the editor's confidence that you're qualified to write this article. You don't want to be too specific, though: If you're querying for an article about "how to tell if you have an ear infection," don't mention that you've recently written another article about "how to tell if you have an ear infection." Instead, give a broader view and say that you've written about health topics for XYZ publication, or that you've already spoken with doctors about this topic.

The second part of this dilemma is whether or not to include similar clips. Again, this will depend on just how similar the rewrite will be. If the material is essentially the same, and you've just repackaged it for a new audience, don't include a clip of the original article. Not only will it lower your chances of an acceptance in the first place, but it will give the editor a reason to pay you a lower fee: He or she will note that you've already been paid to do the research.

Conversely, if the piece is going to touch on significantly different aspects of the topic, or if it expands greatly on a shorter piece, then it's a fine idea to include other, related articles. This should have the opposite effect on an editor: it shows you have expertise about the topic, so you can command a higher fee.

If you are in this business for the long haul, you won't want to pitch a spin-off to a competitor, however. That is, if you wrote your ear infection article for *Health* magazine, and then you sold a similar article to *Women's Health & Fitness*, you'd probably infuriate both editors once they found out you had done so. The editor from *Health* won't hire you again, because she'll believe you're "helping the competition" after she paid you for your work. The editor from *Women's Health & Fitness* won't hire you again, because she'll be afraid you're just going to give her the leftovers of what you already sold to their competitor. So once you've sold an article to a publication, consider its competitors off-limits for an article about the same topic.

Magazines are competitors if their audiences overlap, or if they're competing for the same readers. Let's say you sold the original piece to a parenting magazine that's published only in Florida. Could you pitch a spin-off to another parenting magazine, if it's published only in New York? Absolutely. The people who read the Florida magazine won't also read the New York magazine, so it's perfectly reasonable to sell to both publications.

Keep the question, "How many times can I reprint or resell this piece?" in your mind when you come up with new ideas. Although this may sound crass, just yesterday I had a super inspirational experience that I knew would make a great personal essay, but I didn't make up my mind about whether or not to write it until I decided it would be cost-effective. I watched a boy plunk in quarter after quarter on one of those crane machines where you try to win stuffed animals. He worked hard at it and finally won the object of his desire: a stuffed monkey. Immediately, he handed it to his little sister and gave her a kiss on the forehead. Watching this scene unfold brought tears to my eyes because I had assumed he was trying to win the toy for himself.

I wanted to write that essay. But first I had to think about the odds. It just might sell to a big women's or parenting magazine, I thought—but it might not. It's not a "big" story, just a feel-good little one. I knew I was rolling the dice on getting the piece accepted at a big magazine. But then I realized that regional parenting magazines are among the greatest reprint markets in the world.

There are at least 200 regional parenting magazines in the United States—the kind you'll find free at delis, grocery stores, or area attractions. Generally, they don't pay much, but think about the big picture: Regional magazines need only regional rights, so you can sell the same piece to many, many regional magazines at once.

I cranked out that essay in less than an hour, read it aloud, and to my delight, found that it needed only the slightest tweaking before it was ready to be published. Then I prioritized my list of potential markets. Sure, I'd still like to see it published in a national glossy, so I just sent it off to a few of the major markets. But if they don't bite within a few weeks, the essay will go off to dozens of regional parenting magazines.

I couldn't do that if the story were more idiosyncratic. For example, if my essay was going to be about what the Episcopal religion means to me, I'd know that there were only a few potential markets for this piece, probably none of them high-paying, and no chance of selling it many times over for regional reprinting. So, sure, I might write about it in my journal or write it for low pay one day when I'm between assignments, but that's not where I'm going to focus my efforts. I want to be a factory of ideas that have an excellent chance of bringing me serious paychecks. Don't you?

Building Your Expertise

When I was still relatively new to freelancing, I saw an online call for writers from a new disabilities magazine, asking writers to send résumés, writing samples, and cover letters.

They didn't ask for queries. They didn't seem to want story ideas; they just wanted to find some competent writers so they could make assignments.

Ripe for Reprints

There are certain types of publications that are great candidates for reprints, such as:

➤ *Regional women's magazines*
➤ *Regional bridal magazines*
➤ *Regional sports magazines*
➤ *Regional parenting (and even grandparenting) magazines*
➤ *Small health magazines (check at your YMCA)*
➤ *Newspapers*
➤ *E-zines*

All the better for me: I didn't have any particular idea of what to write about, but I do have a brother with Down syndrome and a strong desire to write for the disabilities market. So I sent off an impassioned letter explaining my background as an advocate for people with disabilities. I tried to convey that I was very interested in writing for them. It was true: In this case, the money was secondary. What I really wanted was the chance to build up my clips in this area, and to write about things that would really matter to me, instead of the dry news articles I'd been writing.

I didn't have appropriate clips for this market, so to prove myself I wrote up a piece as a writing sample. I did a short profile of someone with a disability.

I sent that, along with a clip of a news piece and my résumé.

I didn't mention where the "writing sample" appeared. I didn't tell them that it had never been published. I just said, "Here are two articles of mine."

Sure enough, I received letters back from two editors from that company. The editor-in-chief and the features editor both thought enough of my submission to make sure I'd become a regular contributor.

The pay was pathetic ($50–75 an article), but the assignments were great. They assigned stories that were human interest, little-known, and underreported. I went far beyond what was required of me, interviewing many people and doing extensive research for each story.

At the time, I didn't realize how well it would pay off.

That company eventually stopped using freelancers and hired a full-time staff. I might have been able to get a full-time position, but there's a reason I freelance: I don't want to be stuck in an office all day! I had to move on past the safety net of this low-paying publication, which was probably a good kick in the rear, anyway.

"I've done so much research," I thought. Surely, that had to count for something. What could I do with all these clips and all this new knowledge?

That's when I realized—I had become an expert! I was now a writer who specialized in disabilities issues. I could use that angle to pitch myself to many different venues, and I did.

My first hit from a major women's magazine was the direct result of an assignment from this little publication. I sent off a fresh query for a spin-off article, stating that I had already written about this topic and had access to hundreds of pages of research and interviews. Because of this, I could get the new article to them quickly, and it was all ready for fact-checking.

Next, I chose other publications that might be interested in articles from a "disabilities expert." General interest mags, political mags, women's mags, newspapers, educational mags: You name it, I hit it.

Some of these publications bought re-slanted articles based on the topics I'd already covered, and some gave me new assignments because I had proven myself to be a capable writer in this field.

I wrote about current disabilities issues facing Congress. I wrote profiles for general interest magazines. I wrote "happy ending" stories for women's magazines. All this, based on a low-paying assignment from a web site.

Chapter 10
AND THEY'RE OFF!

Inside This Chapter

- **Submitting ideas to more than one publication**
- **The basics of copyrights**
- **Following up**
- **Keeping track of queries**

You'll never sell anything until you actually start submitting your work. This chapter will cover questions and concerns you may have about sending out your queries.

Simultaneous Submissions

I hear this question a lot: "Can I submit a query about the same topic to more than one market at the same time?"

Absolutely.

You *have* to. If you waited for an answer every time you submitted a query letter, you'd wind up sending out about a dozen letters a year, and landing about two assignments.

Forget it.

Many magazines won't even answer, and most of them will reject your work. Even the most professional freelancers get rejections with far more regularity than they receive acceptances. Therefore, for you to make any kind of reasonable living doing this, you *must* send out queries to several markets at once.

Someone will say, "yes." What then?

Don't panic. This is a good thing, remember? And it doesn't mean you now have to send off apology letters to every other editor, saying you can't write the piece now because it's been accepted elsewhere. Indeed, you should notify *competing* magazines that you must withdraw your query because it has sold, but if the magazines aren't direct competitors, let it play out and see what happens.

My most successful query letter, thus far, has landed me seven original assignments and several reprints. I changed only a few sentences in each query, to "personalize" each one to fit different magazines.

This works because of a few factors: First, I sold first North American serial rights to a print magazine for a feature article about my subject. The piece ran around 1,200 words. Next, another magazine asked for an article. I didn't even mention that I'd already written one: Instead, I asked for a word count and the specifics of what they wanted. As it turned out, they wanted me to concentrate on something completely different from the last article, and only wanted 700 words.

The result was instead of selling a reprint (for much less money), I was able to write the piece completely differently, using the same basic research, without "plagiarizing myself." Similarly, the next five publications each wanted different angles for different markets. One wanted a direct "Q&A"-style interview, another wanted a humor piece, another wanted a first-person essay, one only wanted electronic rights, etc. I never had to tell anyone I used the same query to write all these different articles.

There are only two times you must worry about having the query accepted by more than one venue: if you've queried for something unique (a specific event, observation, or comparison) and cannot think of ways to retell the story in a significantly different way, or if your query is accepted at the same time by competing magazines. In either of those cases, you must tell the second editor that the article has been accepted elsewhere. Be prepared to pitch another idea, and offer to call or write to this editor first the next time you have a great story.

This situation happened to me once: A women's magazine editor contacted me too late, and I had already accepted a competitor's offer. I apologized to the editor, and told her that I would have loved to have written the article for her magazine. She understood that a freelancer's life makes it necessary to have many irons in the fire, and said she wished she'd called me earlier. I said, "If you give me your number, I'd be glad to call you first the next time I have a breaking story."

She did. I haven't used it yet, but you can be sure that the next time I have an idea appropriate for her magazine, her phone will ring. And she may just remember me as the hot writer who got away because she didn't reply fast enough last time.

What If They Steal My Ideas?

I'd like to tell you, unequivocally, that "they" won't. I can't make this guarantee, but what I can tell you is this: it's rare. Any experienced editor knows that it's much more expensive to fight a court battle than it is to pay for an article.

If she likes your idea, most likely, she'll hire you to write the article.

If she likes your idea but thinks you sound incompetent, it's possible that she'll ask to buy the idea, but not the article. This is unusual, but if your idea is excellent, an editor may wish to hire a writer she trusts to execute it. Of course, you can avoid this situation by coming across as a professional who is worthy of her trust. A few magazines such as *Stuff* offer finder's fees for the short FOB sections, not because they don't trust the writers to execute the articles well, but because they say it's not worth it to hire many writers to write lots of little articles when they could just buy the ideas and write them in-house.

Is it worth it for writers? I don't know. In some cases, I'd say "sure," and in others, not a chance. If you don't yet have an impressive bio and clips, then avoid the finder's fees and hold out for the opportunity to get your name and writing in print, even if a quick buck sounds nice. But if you later hook up with a magazine like *Stuff*, knowing in advance that you won't actually be writing these articles, you might set up a sweet deal for yourself by sending them ideas that you don't really want to write about. For example, you might find a great and quirky health study, but that's not really your area. Fine. Pitch it to them as a FOB piece and hope they'll shell out some bucks to take it off your hands.

Rights to Write

A publication may buy several kinds of rights from you:

First North American Serial Rights—The right to publish this piece for the first time in any periodical in North America. All other rights belong to the writer.

One-Time Rights—The nonexclusive right to publish the piece once. The writer can sell the same article to other publications simultaneously.

Second Serial Rights (or Reprint Rights)—Also nonexclusive. Gives the publication the right to reprint an article that has appeared elsewhere.

Electronic Rights—Generally refers to internet publishing. Covers multimedia (CD-ROMs, e-zines, web site content, games, etc.). Get in writing which electronic rights are specified (first electronic, one-time electronic, nonexclusive electronic, archiving rights, etc.).

All Rights—Pretty self-explanatory. You can never sell this piece to anyone else again. Try to avoid this one. Most publications ask for first rights.

Work-for-Hire—The publication/company owns the copyright and doesn't need to give you credit or extra payment, no matter where or when they use your writing. One step worse than all rights.

TV/Motion Picture Rights—Also self-explanatory. Almost always exclusive.

> ### PHONE WARNING
>
> *Don't make a pitch over the phone. Fear of litigation is one of the reasons editors generally won't take phone pitches. The other, of course, is that it's impossible to tell if a person is a good writer based on a phone conversation. It makes me suspicious when a writer feels more comfortable about her phone skills than her writing skills. It's quite easy for a writer to claim that she pitched a story to an editor over the phone and later found that exact story in the magazine. You must establish a paper trail, both for your interest and for the magazine's interest.*

Copyrights

Here's a layman's guide to copyrights:

How does copyright protect my ideas?

It doesn't. Ideas are not subject to copyright. You cannot copyright an idea, a title, a thought, or a concept. You can only copyright the written or recorded form of that idea.

What does this mean to you? Well, it means that an editor *can* legally use ideas you've presented in a query. She cannot, however, use your words. She can't plagiarize the manner in which you've executed your ideas. So, if you've pitched a story about surfing in the Bahamas, and then see an article in the magazine a few months from now about surfing in the Bahamas, you can't cry "foul." If that article contains excerpts from your query, uses the same resources, or is simply a thin rewording of the same pitch you sent, then you have a case.

Your have several options at this point. You can write to the editor and publisher, stating your case and demanding compensation and a written correction with your byline in the next issue. If this isn't satisfactory, you can take the case to Small Claims Court. This is slightly tricky, though—the magazine must either be based in the same state as you reside, or it must be distributed there.

You can also file your grievance with the National Writers Union if you're a member (www.nwu.org). They have many well-trained volunteers on board who can advise you for free, and write letters to the publisher on your behalf.

Finally, if you truly believe your case is iron-tight, you can hire a lawyer. Obviously, you'll have to consider the expense of legal fees, and weigh this against what you stand to gain.

Before you decide you've been ripped off, however, you must consider something:

There's nothing new under the sun.

Unbelievable as it may sound, the odds are that other people have had the exact same amazing idea as you had. It's quite possible that another writer happened to send a very similar query to the editor at about the same time you did. Unless your information was confidential, and there's no way that anyone else would have had access to it, you must accept the possibility that you weren't ripped off—just beaten to the punch.

It's even likely that that's the whole reason you *didn't* get the assignment: A similar article may have already been in the works.

In all the time I've been writing, I've had a query stolen from me only once. And it was stolen by a major women's magazine. What a sad day. The editor had called me the day after I sent my query; she was interested, but wanted to get my subject to sign an exclusivity contract before assigning me the piece. I told her I'd be happy to give her my subject's contact information as long as I knew the assignment was mine if the woman signed. The editor assured me that was the case. So I gave her my subject's attorney's phone and fax number, along with my subject's home phone number. After stringing me along for months with excuses about how they weren't able to get in touch with the attorney, I found out the article had been assigned to someone else—who undoubtedly got the $2,500 I had been promised.

That taught me not to divulge my source's contact information until I had a written contract. I'm currently working with NWU's grievance division on this case, and my advisor explained to me that in a situation like this, I should have demanded a contract that said the assignment was contingent upon the subject signing the exclusivity contract, which would have covered both of our butts, rather than accepting this verbal agreement. I might add that the only reason I did trust the verbal agreement is that it's one of the most popular magazines in America, and I never would have suspected them to be unscrupulous.

Aside from that, I'm still as open as I've ever been. Even though you are taking a small risk, if you don't give editors your trust, you're shooting yourself in the foot. I know writers who refuse to mention names in their queries; for example, they'll say "I plan to interview teen psychologists," whereas I say, "I plan to speak with teen psychologists such as Sally Powers (University of Massachusetts psychology professor who lectures about adolescent depression), Lynn Ponton (author of *The Sex Lives of Teenagers*), and Mike Riera (best-selling author of *Surviving High School*)." Which one inspires more confidence? The other writer sounds like she has no plan and hasn't done any research, whereas I'm showing that I've done my homework and know the experts on my topic.

Does it make it even easier for an editor to take this idea and give it to a staffer, complete with potential interviewees? Yes, but it also makes it easier for her to assign me this piece with confidence, which is what interests me far more.

Do I have to register all my articles with the U.S. Copyright Office?

No. "All original work is automatically entitled to copyright protection the instant it is created and saved in any tangible form (on paper, on disk, on canvas, on film)," says publishing attorney Daniel Steven. You don't need to register it. Also, if your article is published to a copyrighted magazine, your article will be covered under their copyright.

Before your article is published, you may want to protect yourself by having a record of when you wrote it. Your word processing program may automatically "date-stamp" your documents (there will be a "created on" or "last edited on" date imbedded in the document's description). You can also save your articles to disk, organizing articles by month and/or year.

If it's important to you, you can register your works with the U.S. Copyright Office. The forms are available online: www.loc.gov/copyright/forms.

You should be able to use Short Form TX, available for download as a .pdf file. As of this writing, the charge for registration is $20. You do not have to pay a separate fee for each article; instead, you can register a collection of your work (several articles, stories, poems, etc.) together for one copyright registration and one fee. Some writers choose to register groups of their articles twice a year or so.

A few of the editors I've spoken with say it annoys them when a writer submits something with a copyright notice on it. It's almost like proclaiming, "Hey, editor, I don't trust you and want you to see that you can't steal this piece because it's mine, all mine!" All decent editors will assume that the copyright belongs to you. The only time you should include a copyright notice is when you're publishing something on the Web. It discourages would-be plagiarizers from claiming they thought your work was in the public domain.

Do I Need an Agent?

Not at all. Not only would it be extremely unlikely for you to get an agent as a freelance writer, but it probably wouldn't help you one iota, anyway.

If you decide to try longer-form work, such as novels, nonfiction books, or screenplays, then you can think about agents. But if you're planning on sticking to magazines, newspapers, or other short-form publications, agents can actually count as a strike against you, rather than for you.

Why?

Editors want to work directly with you. They don't need the hassle of a middleman. They also know that an agent's job revolves around getting publishers to loosen their purse strings. You'll find that even the most successful freelancers typically handle their own negotiations.

Second, agents aren't interested in most magazine freelancers, since their return rate isn't wonderful. If an agent has to send out your queries, intervene whenever someone wants to hire you, negotiate, draw up contracts, etc., just to get 10 percent of your sales, it's probably not worth her time.

E-Queries

One of the most common questions I get from writers is, "Do e-queries work?" The simple answer is, "You bet." The more complicated answer is, "Usually." Here's why:

There are many benefits to this method. First, you don't have to spend money on postage, ink, paper, and envelopes. Second, response time is faster, on average. Third, if you can find it, you can often send your query straight to the editor of the section of the magazine you want, bypassing the snail mail gatekeepers (assistants and secretaries).

The down side is that email queries do sometimes get ignored. Many big publications frown on this method, because it makes it too easy for writers to deluge their inboxes with idea after idea, and some writers who probably wouldn't bother wasting the stamp have no qualms about dashing off half-baked ideas online.

One trade editor complains that he gets frustrated when a would-be writer doesn't even bother to capitalize or punctuate properly in a query letter. Stephanie Abarbanel of *Woman's Day* says, "A writer I've worked with for five years can knock off an idea and say, 'What do you think, Steph?' Someone I don't know can't do that." I've even gotten queries where the writer abbreviates words like "your" ("yr"), which irritated me to no end—this writer can't be bothered writing the letters "o" and "u" and expects me to trust him with an assignment? Understand that editors are more swamped than ever since writers have taken to the 'Net, and that they now receive more bulk submissions of utterly careless and worthless material from amateurs who take full advantage of the fact that email is free and quick.

Because of this, many publications don't publicize their editors' email addresses. And if there's only one email address listed (like info@nameofmagazine.com), the address is usually meant for general comments or subscription inquiries, and the mail is read by a secretary or webmaster. In that case, email queries often won't be forwarded to the correct person. It's better to ask that secretary/webmaster where you should send your editorial submission rather than just sending the query and hoping he'll forward it to the right person.

However, in my experience, e-queries have worked better than snail mail ones. As long as the publication doesn't specifically state that it will not accept email queries (and even sometimes if it does, if you're feeling gutsy), there's no harm in trying, as long as you don't abuse this "in" by filling the editor's box with all your ideas.

Some editors have even begun encouraging email queries. *Travel + Leisure* prefers e-queries (and sometimes pays more than $1 a word), and *Playboy* happily provides an email address in their guidelines (and pays a minimum of $3,000 for a feature article).

Melissa Walker, freelance writer and editor for *ELLEgirl*, says, "Even if they say snail mail, pitch them via email and offer to send clips [by mail] if they ask for it. Snail mail piles up—and gets rejected by editorial assistants."

This paid off for business and humor writer C.S. Paquin. Her first glossy clip came from a magazine that specifically asked for snail-mail queries. She emailed a personal essay and received an acceptance within four days. It has also paid off for me. I've repeatedly made sales by emailing magazines that ask writers to submit by mail only, and even to magazines that claim not to be open to queries at all!

So, what do you do differently in an e-query compared to a snail-mail query?

You have even less time to engage your reader. A busy editor checks her email with one hand on the mouse, ready to hit "delete." You have to use every word to convince her to read on.

That starts with the subject.

At one time, I would have advised not to put the word "query" in the subject line, because if an editor doesn't like email queries, it's too easy for her to just hit "delete." However, in these days of never-ending spam, it's actually better for you to identify yourself as a writer immediately, rather than risking looking like an ad for "herbal Viagra" or "hot monkey love."

So go ahead and start the subject line with "Query:," then follow it with the topic of the article you're proposing, or the title you have in mind. Examples of subject lines I've used that generated responses: "His Damp Towel, My Pristine Pillowcase," "Yes, Veronica, there is a romantic man," "$310 and a Dream," and "Give Me Back My Foreskin!"

So, you get it. Something that tells the editor this is an interesting email.

If you're mailing out the same letter to many recipients, be careful not to let it show! Do not, under any circumstances, use the "copy to" or "blind copy to" option to list several addresses. Each letter must appear to be tailor-made to that publication, even if it's just a matter of changing a few words.

Include the name of the magazine or section somewhere in your query; for example, "I propose a 500-word article for your 'Tools Rule' section."

Always make sure you've included your address and phone number in the query, even if you expect they'll respond via email. If the editor gets excited about your letter, you don't want to let her excitement cool down while she goes through the rest of her mail and prepares to write back. Give her the option to pick up the phone immediately and give you that assignment!

> *Cracking the Code*
>
> *If you can't find the specific email address you need, see if you can find ANY email address for someone at the magazine. (Often, you'll find an email address listed for the person in charge of advertising.) Check to see how that address is formatted.*
>
> *If it looks like this: jsmith@nameofmagazine.com, then you can guess the format for emails is first initial, last name@nameofmagazine.com. If you know the department editor's name is Melissa Jones, then try sending your letter to mjones@nameofmagazine.com.*
>
> *If it looks like this: John_Smith@nameofmagazine.com, then you can guess the format is first name_last name@nameofmagazine.com, and format your letter to Melissa_Jones@nameofmagazine.com.*

Be an Email Detective

Many magazines have a corresponding web site. Go there, and search for a "staff" page, a masthead, an "about our company" or a "contact" page. Many list individual email addresses. Rather than firing off a letter to the editor-in-chief, try to find the address for the particular department editor who handles articles like yours. She's likely less swamped with queries, and you're more likely to get an answer.

Sometimes, it's just a matter of experimentation before you figure out the appropriate email address. Most companies employ one of the following methods:

Firstname_Lastname@magazine.com

firstinitallastname@magazine.com

firstname.lastname@magazine.com

Firstname@magazine.com

Lastname@magazine.com

position@magazine.com (try "editor@magazine.com" if all else fails)

If you're willing to invest a little time wading through "undeliverable" emails that come back to you, you may just hit the right person with a little effort. This has paid off for me more than once.

For example, I really wanted to break into Salon.com. I had seen a general submissions address on their site—probably query@salon.com or something similar. It said that the queries would be routed to the appropriate editors. I dashed off a perfect query, and didn't hear a word back.

Bummed, but not defeated, I tried again about a month later, with a brand new query. Again, not a word.

Then I found the staff page, and located the address for the editor of the department that would be most appropriate for my idea. I went back into my files and fished out that first query letter. (This was about six months after I'd sent the first query.) I peeked through it again and decided I had to give it a second shot. Literally 10 minutes after I sent off the query, I got a note back from the editor, telling me he was interested in the piece and wanted to hear more about it. He even asked if I could turn it into a daily diary for the site.

As life would have it, he didn't end up buying the piece, but he was impressed with my writing, and asked me to submit again.

Feeling more confident, I then sent a query to another editor at Salon, and scored. Sometimes, when you know your writing belongs at a certain publication, you have to keep hammering away at the keys until the gatekeepers let you in.

More recently, I got sick of wasting stamps querying *Woman's Day* and *Good Housekeeping*. I spent about 15 minutes guessing at email addresses using the aforementioned formulas, and wound up getting my queries to the right editors. I received responses from both within a week. Neither editor complained about the fact that I'd e-queried or asked how I got their email addresses, and in fact, one offered me a contract. It takes an awful lot to convince me to send a postal mail query anymore; I'd have to *really* want to break into the magazine and know that e-queries weren't acceptable to any of the appropriate editors.

If we're talking about how to make more money as a freelance writer—which is, after all, the topic of this book—I'd advise you to take the same approach. Sending e-queries saves you money and time, and it often helps you get past the gatekeepers. Perhaps best of all, it's much more likely that you'll get a personalized response, even if it is a rejection letter.

When an editor at *House Beautiful* rejected one of my essays by email, she told me that she thought the essay should be published, and even suggested which magazines might buy it. Would she have done that by postal mail? I doubt it.

What About Faxes?

Nope. In my experience, faxes generally are not well-received. They tie up the line on the other end, don't always come through clearly, and rarely end up in the right hands. Stick to email and snail mail.

What Happens to My Query?

If you sent it by mail, it'll likely be read by an editorial assistant or intern. He may reject it outright, or he may pass it along to the appropriate editor. (If you've e-queried, you can usually bypass that.) If the editor likes it, it will probably end up on the list of subjects to talk about at the next editorial meeting.

Each magazine's methods are different, but on the whole, editorial meetings are held weekly, biweekly, or monthly. The time to discuss potential articles is short. Melissa Walker, who has worked as an editor for *ROSIE* and *ELLEgirl*, says, "I've never been to an editorial meeting where actual queries were read aloud. It's more like editors bringing their own list of ideas (some queried, some self-generated) and rattling them off. An editor-in-chief gives you 10 seconds to sell each story (if that)."

In general, that editor-in-chief must approve each article that will be assigned, so it's rare for a section editor to have the authority to accept your query letter without getting permission.

In an article for *Library Culture*, Daniel G. Kipnis writes that *People* magazine has a weekly editorial meeting. "An executive editor runs the meeting and since the staff is on a deadline the meeting runs quickly and efficiently (averaging 30 minutes). The managing editor runs through the mark ups of each page of the to-be-released issue to confirm that the layout is finished and to address any final inquiries. In addition, the meeting is used as a brief brainstorming session for future issues."

Notice the word "brief." Assuming that editors really do have about 10 seconds to pitch each idea, what will the editors say about your article?

Well, let's hope you wrote a fantastic lead, because there's a good shot that this 10-second pitch will sound a whole lot like the first sentence or two of your pitch. You can make this editor's job a lot easier by keeping this editorial meeting in mind when you write your queries; what can you write that will be easy to summarize in just a few seconds?

Once the editor-in-chief makes a decision, it's final. It doesn't matter how much that section editor loved your query; if the editor-in-chief isn't bowled over, it's back to the drawing board unless there's a compelling reason to consider that idea again later. For example, if something makes it newsworthy or if the writer's credits vastly improve, it might get a second shot. I had queried *Creative Screenwriting* for a profile of screenwriter John Fusco and hadn't heard a word back. A year later— yes, a *year*—the editor emailed to assign me the piece. Why? Because John had a new Disney movie coming out. He wrote *Spirit: Stallion of the Cimarron*, which was getting some good buzz. That editor had held onto my query letter all that time, and when he heard about John's new movie, he remembered me.

Now, *Creative Screenwriting* isn't the same as, say, *Parade*. An editor at *Parade* isn't likely to remember a query she read a year ago. So it's perfectly okay to write to an editor if you have a compelling reason why she should look at your query again. This, of course, does not mean you should write a month later and say, "Hey, I got another publication credit. Now do you want to reconsider?" It also doesn't mean you should desperately look for news connections that are threadbare. If your article is about coping with divorce, don't write to your editor to point out that a celebrity couple is getting divorced, so now would be a good time to run that article of yours. On the other hand, if your article is about the various types of food poisoning and there's news of a sudden outbreak of E. coli contamination at a fast food joint, making hundreds of people sick, that's a more legitimate reason to ask the editor to take another look at your amended query.

When Should I Follow Up?

Although it depends on whom you ask, I would advise you not to spend too much energy on follow-ups. In general, if you don't receive an answer within about a month, that means "no." Some bigger companies may hold on to queries they like and present them at editorial meetings, in which case, your pitch may sit around for a few months. However, most queries are read within the week they arrive, and most are tossed about 20 seconds after they're opened. If an editor is interested and planning to hold onto your query, she'll likely let you know within that month, because she doesn't want to take the risk that you'll go sell it somewhere else in the meantime.

Calling an editor to ask if she's had time to think about your query yet is futile. If you sent it by mail, your query was probably read by an assistant. Even if the assistant gave it to her, or if she read it herself, it was likely among hundreds of other queries she read that week. And thousands she read over the past couple of months. And tens of thousands she's read over the past couple of years. Unless your query really stood out, she won't remember it.

It's very unlikely that you'll get through to an editor over the phone, anyway. A secretary or assistant may take your message, but again, unless the editor is interested in your piece, she won't call you back.

Following up by mail means you get the grand opportunity to waste two more stamps and get a paper cut on your tongue.

A quick email follow-up is okay. Sometimes there are legitimate reasons why an editor never saw your query: For example, if you sent it by email, it might have been gobbled up by her spam filter. And sometimes the opposite happens: I sent a story to a U.K. publication by email. The editor expressed interest and we were negotiating a price. Then I didn't hear from him again for weeks. Finally, I followed up to ask what happened, and he told me, "I emailed you twice and was wondering why you weren't answering me!" He forwarded me the emails, and sure enough, my dumb ISP just never got those messages through to me. My mailbox was overloaded, but they didn't tell me, and they didn't send bounceback messages to the hapless people who thought I was ignoring them.

Here are the situations in which I think following up is always appropriate:

➤ *If you received some kind of request or response in the first place.*
If you queried because an editor asked you to, or if you queried and someone wrote back to let you know that they were interested or considering your proposal, then you should follow up. Give at least two weeks after your last correspondence, then follow up with an email or phone call.

➤ *If this is a market you've dealt with before.*
If you've written for this editor before, he should have the courtesy to respond to your next query. If via email, give at least two weeks before checking in. If via snail mail, a month.

➤ *If you're absolutely dying to work for this market.*
Do you really think your work is perfect for a particular publication, but can't seem to get an answer from them? Drop in a polite note explaining this. You might write something along these lines:

> **Dear Ms. Smith:**
>
> **I'm writing to check in to make sure you received my proposal, "Traveling Europe on a Shoestring Budget," sent May 2nd. I'm eager to hear your response, as I would love the opportunity to write for *Your Mag*. I am a faithful reader of the magazine and an experienced travel writer, and believe I can offer a piece that fits well with *Your Mag's* spirit.**
>
> **I would appreciate it if you would let me know if you've had time to consider my proposal. Thanks for your time.**

Not all writers take the same lax approach to following up as I do, however. Kelly James-Enger, contributing editor for magazines such as *Energy for Women* and *Oxygen*, says she always follows up. "I used to follow up by mail," she says. "Now I usually either email or call after two to four weeks, depending on the circumstances."

Karen Asp, fitness columnist for *Allure* and freelancer for magazines such as *Fitness*, *Shape*, and *Family Circle*, also follows up on every query. "I rarely phone because I know editors are extremely busy," she says. "Instead, I email. How soon after I've submitted depends on the publication. However, if I have an especially hot topic, I'll follow up faster, perhaps within the week."

Most publications offer an approximate response time in their *Writer's Market* listings. Overeager writers sometimes forget how many queries an editor gets, or how much planning goes into each issue to determine which articles fit in which sections of which issues. Department editors usually have to present your query to the editor-in-chief, and as *Ladies' Home Journal* editor Chandra Czape says, it might take six weeks for her editor-in-chief to make a decision once Chandra has presented it to her. Sometimes, editors take care of all queries once a month. There can be many causes for delay in responses.

Following up must be done professionally and sparingly. Even if you're hurt and frustrated and mad at an editor for not answering you, skip the guilt trips ("Well, since I still haven't heard from you, I guess that means you're not interested") and the scolding ("It has been far longer than your indicated response time"). Never hound an editor who isn't responding. Think whatever you like, complain about it to your friends and your cat, but don't make an editor remember you as the writer who kept pestering her while she was in the middle of 12 different crises. And if you follow up and get a rejection, be sure to thank the editor for checking into the matter for you, anyway.

Should I Keep on Clippin'?

Let's say you sent a query with clips to an editor at *Autoweek*. He rejected it. A few weeks later, you decide to send another query. Do you need to send your clips again? Absolutely. Even at small magazines, it would be highly, highly unlikely for an editor to be able to remember what your clips were like. But where to draw the line?

I've sometimes had trouble deciding exactly how many times to keep sending those clips. I mean, you *will* come to a point where an editor is familiar with you, even if he hasn't given you an assignment yet. If you've been sending an editor a query a month all year long with those same clips, well . . . first of all, it's time to vary your clips (if possible, don't send the same group of clips to the same editor more than twice, or the editor may worry that's all you have), but second of all, if you're now on a friendly basis with the editor, it's probably okay to drop the clips, unless you publish something new that you're dying to show him.

When I've come to the stage where I'm pretty sure the editor remembers me and knows I'm a good writer, instead of trying to find new clips to send every time, I add in a note like this: "I've sent my clips before, but if you'd like to see them again, please let me know."

Do I Need to Keep Records?

It's essential that you keep track of your queries and submissions. While you may be able to spout out the names of every editor who's ever shown a morsel of interest in you when you're just starting out, once you've sold dozens, hundreds, or even thousands of articles, it all gets a bit fuzzy.

You will regret it later if you have failed to note the name of that editor who asked you to submit again, or if you forgot to keep track of what rights you've sold on an article. So take the time now to set up a tracking system. You'll be glad you did.

Track 'Em, Danno

When querying, you'll want to keep track of where you've sent your ideas, how, when, and to whom. This serves many purposes: For example, let's say you sent an e-query to an editor at *SmartMoney Magazine*. If you didn't write this down, how are you going to know if/when to follow up, and which editor to follow up with? But let's say you did write this down. You look, and you notice you sent this query by email six weeks ago. Now you have a few choices: You can resend it with a note saying you're just making sure it got through, send it by snail mail instead, send it to a different editor, or you can assume it's a rejection and move on.

If you check your records and see that a certain query has been rejected over and over, it might be a sign that it's time to rework that query. If you see that a certain editor has rejected your work over and over, it might be a sign that it's time to try a different editor. You'll also get a better feel for each editor's response time, and you'll be able to see at a glance which editors gave you some kind of encouragement to try again.

Keeping track of where you found a market is a smart idea, too. For example, once when I proposed an article to an e-zine, it took them several months to respond to me, but they did respond with an interest. They wanted me to expand my query to include more research. I thought, "Hmm. If I know they pay well, no problem. But if they're a low-paying publication, I shouldn't put in the extra time."

The problem was that I had forgotten to note where I found the market. I searched all over the web to try to dig up this e-zine's guidelines and pay rates, but came up empty. I checked my market books . . . nothing. I wound up spending hours looking through every writers' newsletter I had gotten in the past six months before finally stumbling upon a listing that told me the market paid about $50 per article: not enough to make it worth my time to write a highly-researched piece.

Now I remember to make simple notes when I find a potential market: When I send the query, I include something like: "Absolute Markets 10/9." This tells me that the market's guidelines were in the October 9th issue of the Absolute Markets newsletter, so if I want to check back on it in the future, I'll know where to find it. This also helps me if I want to query this market again—I know where to go to re-read the guidelines to make sure my future ideas are appropriate for them.

I currently use the submission tracking feature at WritersMarket.com (which comes with a paid subscription) to record all of these details, but you don't need to do that. You can make charts to include in your notebook, index card files, or make your own submission tracking forms on the computer.

You can use the following chart as a simple model.

My Query Records

Idea	Suitable market	Name and email address of editor	Where I found this market	Date I sent query	Method of query	Response

In addition to keeping records of where your queries have gone, it's also very smart to keep an index card file of any additional information you attain from trade publications or conversations with editors and other writers.

This way, you can avoid making the kind of annoying mistake I did. I read in *Writer's Market* that *Writer's Digest* was in need of first-person essays about the writing life for their "Chronicles" column. I had a story I knew they couldn't refuse, so I wrote it up and sent it.

A few days letter, I received a letter from the editor that said while the essay was great, they had discontinued the column in their magazine, and although they planned to reincarnate it on their web site, it would be a much lower word count and lower pay.

Why was it such a foolish mistake? Because I had heard that tidbit about a month before the editor wrote me that letter, and I failed to write it down. Another writer mentioned it on a bulletin board somewhere, and I simply forgot about it until I saw that letter. Now I looked foolish for submitting the column, because it showed that I hadn't read the most current issue, and I wasted valuable hours of my time writing an article for a defunct column. If I had kept better records, I would have flipped to the card for *Writer's Digest*, noticed the change, and skipped that piece.

Other things to note on your cards once you've gotten an assignment: Was the editor receptive to negotiations? Did you find any differences between what was offered to you versus what was listed in the guidelines or *Writer's Market* listing? Did the editor mention any other needs the publication may have? Did she send you a style sheet? Did she share any personal interests or information with you?

Also, anytime you find out that an editor, pay rate, sections, format, or subject matter of a publication has changed, be sure to note it.

In addition, I keep a filing cabinet for all of my freelance work. In it, I have folders marked for every publication for which I've written. I keep copies of all contracts and correspondence in the folders, plus any research and interview notes I've done for the articles. I also have folders for markets I'd like to query soon, and I keep a small notebook where I record outstanding invoices, then check them off when payment is received. At a glance, I can see who's overdue and how much I earned in a particular month.

Keeping good records comes in handy when you want to query a publication you've worked for in the past. First, it allows you to remember the name and contact information of the person who hired you before. It may also remind you of a personal fact or common ground to use in your next contract.

Just as importantly, it will remind you of the terms you got last time. If your first piece earned you $0.50 a word, and they were happy with the piece, you may want to negotiate yourself a raise to $0.60 or $0.70 a word with the next piece. Or, if you were paid on publication last time, you may consider asking for "on acceptance" this time. Review the last piece you wrote for them and notice how it differs from the published version. Did they cut down your word count? Take out your witty remarks? These are all things to consider when gearing up for your next query.

You may find it unnecessary to have an extensive filing system in the beginning. A few binders and folders should suffice until they begin to bulge. Whatever you do, don't let lack of space stop you from keeping accurate records of your work.

How Long Will It Take?

Karen Asp, who has a bio that many writers would envy, including credits from most major women's and health magazines, says her freelancing success didn't happen overnight. Instead, it took "tons of luck, tears, and sweat, and then some! I was also persistent. As soon as I got a ding, I turned around and sent that editor another idea. Finally, I bit my nails and learned how to be patient."

Her patience paid off. Karen got her big break when she caught wind of a study about eating disorders that hadn't gotten press attention yet. She pitched it to *Shape*, they bought it, and "once that door opened, others began crumbling," she says.

Most new writers don't break into a magazine on their first shot, says Jennifer Nelson, who also writes for most of the top women's and health magazines. The freelancers who land assignments have usually paid their dues studying and pitching ideas for that magazine. "Pay attention to how close you are actually coming," she says. "When editors email you to say they like the idea but it's just not right or they've done something similar recently or have something like it in the works—you know you are right on the edge of landing work."

Jennifer says there are top editors all over the country who know her only from her pitches and clips; she hasn't written for them yet, but they now recognize her name and even comment on her work when they see it in other publications. "One editor at a major home and garden publication writes 'keep the ideas coming' routinely—yet I haven't landed a single assignment with the publication yet."

Some writers would throw in the towel, but like Jennifer, I have learned that once an editor gets to know your name and see several of your pitches, she's often waiting for you to send her that irresistible one that will allow her to give you a shot. Editors don't typically encourage writers who they don't plan to work with, so if you've gotten any kind of personal response or positive feedback from an editor, consider it a good sign that she considers you a contender for a spot in the magazine.

"Persistence pays off. Keep sending your pitches and eventually the right one will hit. Problem is, most writers give up long before they get to that stage," says Jennifer.

More Questions

If you have other questions, don't be afraid to turn to your fellow writers for help. If you have the email address of an experienced freelancer, use it. Don't expect hours of free mentoring, but a couple of quick questions shouldn't bother anyone. In this field, I have been pleasantly surprised to find that the top freelancers are often the nicest and most generous ones. Most don't mind fielding questions for writers who genuinely want to make their submissions the best they can be.

You can also ask your questions on discussion lists and message boards for writers, such as mine at http://pub43.ezboard.com/babsolutewrite. Be aware that some inexperienced writers love to spout out advice, too, so not every response you get will be perfect, but if you take the time to know your fellow forum visitors, you'll quickly learn who gives good advice and who doesn't. Just remember to do the same for someone else when *you're* the top freelancer!

Chapter 11

SOLD!

Inside This Chapter

- **Payment schedules**
- **Bios**
- **The pros and cons of spec writing**
- **Negotiating**
- **Submitting your article**

The Sales

Okay, you sent out your killer query, and an editor called you with the big news: You got the assignment! Congratulations, you! Go on and do a little dance of joy, then crash back to reality with your new mantra:

"GET IT IN WRITING."

Make sure the editor tells you that a written contract is forthcoming in the near future. If the editor doesn't bring it up, then you bring it up. At the end of the conversation, just say, "Great! Thanks for the assignment. So . . . are you going to send me the contract by mail, or do you want to send it by email or fax instead?"

If you've researched your market, you probably already have an idea of the pay rate, but be sure to cover this ground during that initial phone call if the editor fails to mention it. Here are some important points to remember regarding payment:

Payment on Publication vs Payment on Acceptance

Many markets want to pay you on publication of your article rather than on acceptance of your article. This can be a problem for the writer, because many magazines and journals have long lead times (a long time between when they assign you the article and when it actually ends up in print). If you write an article in January, and it doesn't get published until November, you probably won't see a check until December.

Worse, they may accept your article, but later decide to bump it. Recently, an editor of mine told me there had been a "change in management" and that an article I wrote (which I had worked on for nearly two months) would not run, after all. I was tremendously lucky that I was paid on acceptance months ago; otherwise, I might have just lost $4,000 of income!

Payment schedule is a point on which you can negotiate. You can ask for payment within 30 days of submission, but be aware that very few publications will agree to this. The best alternative is to negotiate for payment on acceptance. The editor may claim she hasn't had time to read and approve the article until a week before it goes to the printer, anyway, but it does give you a much better shot at timely payment. If this is refused, it gives you a little leverage to work with on the other issues, such as kill fees, bios, sidebars, and photos.

Kill Fees

If you get the assignment, and, for whatever reason, an editor decides not to print your article, you can still receive partial payment if you've negotiated a kill fee. This is generally between 25 and 50 percent of the sale price. If you are offered $800 to write an article, you may get a $200–400 kill fee. It's a well-known fact that big publications "kill" articles all the time. Some editors admit to assigning 10–20 percent more than they could ever fit in their magazines. They do this so they can pick and choose from the final products, or so they can see how things fit once the layout is complete. Some articles will be pushed back to other issues, and some will just be trashed.

Think of a kill fee as a prenuptial agreement with a spouse you don't really trust. Tacky? Get over it. Unless you've worked with the publisher many times before (and sometimes even then), you can't trust anyone to be "fair." Even well-intentioned editors and publishers run into financial trouble, get fired, change jobs, or change issue themes. Think about how you'll feel after researching, writing, and perfecting an article, only to find out that it's been cut and you won't receive a dime.

If your contract says you'll be paid on submission or acceptance, you should be paid no matter what, as long as your article isn't rejected due to qualitative reasons (that is, the editor thinks your piece stinks and can't be salvaged). The only reason you need a kill fee in this situation is as insurance: Just in case that editor *does* think your article stinks, you still want to get paid for your time.

If it says you'll be paid on publication, the kill fee is of even more importance. There are many reasons your article may not wind up being published, even if it's exactly what you promised to deliver, so the kill fee